IDEAS HAVE LEGS

CONTENTS

CONTENTS

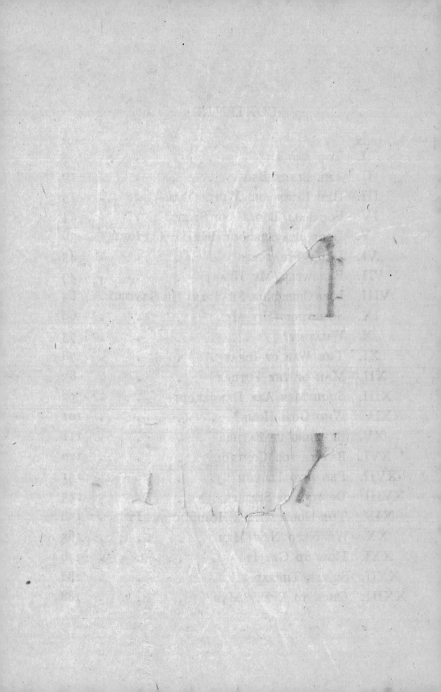

CHAPTER I

YOU AND I

WE are alive, you and I, in an age when millions dream of death.

Never, since man started to run the world God made, has human agony been organised by humans for humans with such science and success.

But something men have yet to learn. We cannot put breath back into one of the millions of bodies we destroy.

It is our bodies, yours and mine, which enable us to talk together though we may never have met. The sinews of your hand contract and grip this page. The nerves of your eyes send the message of the print back to that three pounds of liquid, membrane and matter encased in its narrow bony cavern of the skull, which is called your brain.

The sinews of my hand grasp and direct the pen— first softly into the inkpot—then in whirls, strokes, dots and intervals across the paper. My eyes hover over the sheet like aircraft spotting for distant artillery. They wireless back a stream of information to my three-pound ration of marshy, trembling grey matter, so that the brain is able to control correctly the shape, size and sequence of the letters by which its thoughts are conveyed from me to you.

So here we sit, you in your chair, I in mine. We travel with certainty towards each other's minds and hearts by means of our bodies. For these bodies of ours are machines infinitely more complicated and competent than any which man has devised for their destruction. But we live so close to them that we miss the miracle.

We are fearfully and wonderfully made. Chemists tell us that our bodies are water, potash, iron, phosphates, which can be bottled, labelled and shelved. But the story does not end at that point. There is something inside that body of ours which cannot be accounted for by the water and the chemicals which compound our frame.

It is that something which makes you *understand* the print which your brain and eye can only make you *see*. Our arms and legs, brains, hands and eyes will one day disintegrate and scatter again into the elements, to swell the multitudinous ocean, to travel the clouds and be dust and dirt in cities we have never known. Yet there is a faith in man which tells him that the *something* is there which is for ever his and his own responsibility.

We know each other, you and I. There is that something in both of us which can allow us to touch hearts without touching hands.

I, like you, have felt my heart lift at the beauty of green fields, and the sound of wind through trees.

I have loved the taste of food. I have spread and stretched my body to the warmth of sunshine and of fires.

I have felt pain, and the peace when pain is ended. I have known fear and also the shame which makes the frightened man keep silent lest others sense his secret.

I have shivered with the cold and spoken in the heat of that rage which hurts, enjoys the hurting and later fruitlessly regrets. I have lusted and quarrelled, slept and loved and toiled, met the gay days and the grey days in their marching cavalcade.

Death has touched me with his strange hand. Life too, with his finger of mystery, when my children puckered their faces and whimpered their first breath.

We are brother and sister, you and I, companions in a journey and comrades in a crusade. Young or old, rich or poor, female or male, handsome or ugly, drunk or dry, we are the ordinary men and women of the nation. We are part of its past.

We are its future too. Through the power of people will a new age stir and be born. No new age has been born any other way.

For within the framework of men's bodies is generated the most powerful explosive force known in history—the explosive force of ideas.

Frail children of dust we are and feeble as frail. The commonest knife will end the noblest life. Yet from and through our minds are born ideas which conquer the skies, break and remake nations, explore the abysses of the ocean and measure the heats and vapours of the uttermost planets in the universe.

The idea conceived and born by the passion of one heart can shape and change the lives of millions, leading great nations on to destruction or to destiny. We have seen it happen more than once in our own lifetime.

Ideas are on the march in the world to-day, as well as armies. Ideas move faster than armies. They travel ahead of them as well as behind them. They need no ships to cross the seas, neither will fortifications keep them beyond a frontier.

Ideas to transform history are bidding for the hearts of all humanity to-day. There is the idea that one class should dominate, or that one section should dominate, or that one race should dominate or that one group of nations should dominate.

Yet in the end all these ideas will fail. For there is one idea destined to master all others in this day and age —to establish in our lifetime the fresh, brave world for which all openly long, and in which few wholeheartedly believe.

Chapter II

THE BLACK BAG

IDEAS change men. Ideas shape nations. So many ideas bid for the allegiance of each human heart as it takes its journey from the womb to the tomb. And when millions of ordinary men and women begin to follow the same star history is moulded.

A hundred years from now when the pain and tears and blood are only a shadow, and the outline of events is clearly and coldly seen, an historian will attach more importance to the ideas which grip men and alter the character of nations after a war than to the war itself. He will see that war is a symptom of the disease of an age rather than the disease.

What great forces and ideas gripped the lives of millions of men after 1918 and turned them down the road which led to disaster?

In order to settle that question, we need to take a sample of an age and examine the moulding and shaping of events upon it during those inter-war years.

So I put myself in the black bag. I am like the barley which farmers carry in their small black bags of silk to market. When a farmer has barley heaped within his barn, he bares his arm and plunges it full length into the cool, yielding heart of the grain. He brings out a handful. Into the bag it goes, and off to market for the inspection of the merchant.

I am a fair sample to choose. For I am so typical a product of our age. Between the wars my character was carved.

These incidents of my life are of the stuff which makes

the character of millions—tears and triumph, exertion and exhaustion, love and hate, folly and fun, poverty and prosperity, laughter and laziness and drive. Ordinary things in ordinary men which settle the fate of nations.

The most ordinary thing about me is the fact that for many years I prided myself on being a little bit out of the ordinary—more intelligent than many, nicer than most and with qualities which, although the rest of the world might not wholly assess them, I myself fully appreciated.

Like most ordinary people, I have memories of childhood. And one of them has a part in this tale. That memory is a man. His name was Arthur and he was my uncle.

Uncle Arthur was of lean and tempered steel. He was blue-eyed and blond, unlike the other black-browed, tough-hided Howards. He was a hero of my childhood, so gay and so gallant. He was a magnificent footballer and the crowds roared as he swept forward with the ball.

Once he set me on his back and ran with me down the street, so I felt the air rush by and a sense of peril and yet of escape from the world, as if I were borne forward in the crow's-nest of a tall-masted and lithe ship through tumbling seas. It was a relief and a regret when Uncle Arthur set me down. I said, "Again, Uncle, again," and then gulped with apprehension as he gripped and hoisted me aloft.

Uncle Arthur went off to France to fight the Germans. I saw him in uniform before he sailed away. He seemed an indestructible conqueror to my childhood gaze.

The family had given him a patent body-shield. This was a steel waistcoat, proof against bullets and shell splinters. It covered a man from the neck down to the small of the back. Uncle Arthur made jokes about it before he said good-bye.

Unforgettable, unforgotten, those good-byes of 1914–1918 when a generation of youth and strength and daring went away and a million fewer came back home again.

I remember, I remember, as a child.

The trains full of troops pulling out and the trains full of wounded pulling in as dusk fell.

The feverish cheers and hectic laughter under the grime and steam and smoke.

The songs "It's a Long Way to Tipperary", "Pack Up Your Troubles", "Keep the Home Fires Burning"— the potency of such music to tear the heart. These were the last words so many mothers, wives, daughters heard their menfolk sing as the trains, slowly but with gathering speed, disappeared South into the darkness.

The sudden silence after the troop trains had departed —all conversation ceased, no need now to pretend to be cheerful so as to send the boys off with the memory of a smile—the huddles and clusters of women, the strength and resolution and glory of Britain, standing silent for a moment or two straining their eyes after the red tail-lights of the trains, then turning and quietly, quickly, heads down, slipping off through the barriers towards their empty homes.

There was a dignity and a poignancy about those Southern Railway platforms in the last war, a sense of sacrifice and dedication which even a child could feel. I believe it was the thousands of unknown tears and prayers sent up from brave hearts which gave an atmosphere of consecration to those places.

Uncle Arthur and a sergeant were out one night on patrol in No Man's Land. Someone from the German lines fired a Very Light. Uncle Arthur and the sergeant lay still on the ground. A shell exploded nearby. Presently the sergeant said, "It's all right, sir, we can get up now."

Uncle Arthur answered, "I'm trying to get up, Sergeant, but I can't seem to manage it." And indeed he never stood on his feet again in this world, though he was nigh seven years a-dying. They wheeled him to an emergency hospital in a barrow. A piece of shrapnel had severed his spine. The shrapnel was the size of half a lump of sugar.

It had penetrated his spine about half-way down, just at the point where the covering of the body-shield would have been most adequate.

But Uncle Arthur was generous as well as gay. That night on patrol it had been the sergeant's turn to wear the body-shield.

Never again of his own volition did Uncle Arthur move the lower half of his body.

It is a sombre spectacle for a child to see a living man disintegrate year by year, week by week, day by day. Uncle Arthur's lower half shrivelled to the proportion of a mummy during his own lifetime, those valiant legs which had kicked and run and leapt to the clamour of applauding multitudes. So shrunken was that mighty man of valour.

He died.

Most families in the world have the savagery and sadness of war focussed for them by some personal tragedy like that of my Uncle Arthur.

I grew up between two wars. I disliked war. I perceived its futility. I believed that Uncle Arthur had fought in the war to end wars and that therefore war could not be for me. So I did nothing effective about it.

I disapproved of it in my heart and with my mind. I thought that was adequate. I imagined that war was something which, if enough people did not like it, just did not happen. It was a tragic mistake. The majority of the earth did not like war. But war came again.

I believed for some time in the League of Nations because that body enunciated all the vague aspirations and ideals, many of them fine in themselves, for which I stood, without calling upon me personally to do anything sacrificial about them.

I never realised, in those inter-war years, that goodwill in a man or a nation is no answer to self-will in a man or nation. For one is a state of mind, the other is a force. When a force meets a state of mind, the state of mind is brushed aside with violence.

For while I and millions like me in Britain were from time to time vaguely enthusiastic about the necessity for ending certain things we did not like, our country had no faith big enough to kindle the hearts of every citizen to action. But in other parts of the world millions of men were on the march for new beliefs.

Somewhere the other side of No Man's Land, on the night Arthur was hit, a lonely and self-centred artist crouched in a trench. He was a corporal. His name was Adolf Hitler.

He formed an idea. He ate, slept, toiled, lied and fought for it. It was such a fire in the heart of this unknown man that it inflamed millions, shook civilisation and made inconclusive the courage and sacrifice of Arthur's generation.

The power of Hitler's idea restored strength for a time to Germany, made her probably the most hated nation on earth, shattered the old order so it can never be the same again, sentenced men, women and children all the world over to suffering beyond human power to realise, and at one point came within touch of triumph.

CHAPTER III

RED LENIN AND WHITE TIES

HITLER'S idea was not the only big idea to burst upon mankind as a result of the 1914–1918 conflict. It was not the only big idea on the march as I and millions like me grew to manhood.

For in 1917 the Germans discovered a secret weapon which, by a single explosion, put one of their most formidable enemies out of the war.

This secret weapon was packed inside the domed head of Vladimir Ilyich Ulyanov, known to the world as Lenin. The decisive and disintegrating effect of his big idea upon the framework of a nation was so well understood and so greatly feared by the Germans that they sealed Lenin in a train on his passage through their country from Switzerland and smuggled him into Russia. He created a revolution there which changed for ever the shape of that land.

Lenin's idea is one of the most powerful of the new ideas which are on the march to-day. It has gained spectacular success. Out of that sealed train in 1917 stepped a man whose concentrated passion towards a single objective has penetrated, to a greater or less extent, within the structure of every nation in the world, working like yeast to agitate and stir and unsettle the existing order.

When Lenin was seventeen years old they hanged his brother for attempting to kill the Czar. Lenin began to hate. This fanatical genius of the hard, brilliant mind and the ruthless spirit smouldered with loathing against the power and wealth of the Czar, which had destroyed

his brother. He decided to replace the rule of one class
by the rule of another class.

He looked around and saw the hatred of the masses
against the Czar so bitter that when the Czar took a railway journey, paid soldiers had to be posted along the
track to guard against accidents.

He saw luxury and delicate social graces in the midst of
starvation, corruption and cruelty.

He saw high "Society" urging Christian morality upon
the masses and accepting low farmyard morals for
itself.

And with a dynamic energy and ability which has
seldom been equalled in human history, which has rattled
the walls of the world and may yet pull nations down,
he set himself to the task of creating chaos so that his idea
of a new world order might arise from it.

He knew it was a tremendous task. But he was a
tremendous human force. He said, "The dictatorship
of the proletariat is a relentless struggle waged with
bloodshed, a war a hundred times more difficult, more
long drawn out, more complicated than the most blood-
thirsty war which could be possible between nations."

Lenin is embalmed. You can still see that quarter-
moon moustache, that calculating, colossal forehead and
that rocky jaw preserved by chemicals in Moscow
against the attack of decay. But his living memorial is
the momentum of his idea in the world he has quit,
rather than in the cold and mummified lineaments
preserved by those who, as a result of his passion, knew
no other god to worship.

Lenin's idea had its attraction for me, as I suppose it
had to a greater or less extent for millions in that inter-
war period. Often I felt bitter and spoke bitterly about
the miseries of the poor in my own country, one of the
richest in the world. At a time when the unemployment

figures in Great Britain were near the three million mark, I travelled the mining villages where for generations brave men have sweated in darkness and danger to keep the fires and furnaces of this nation aflame.

In one street I saw twenty or thirty children playing. I stopped to watch them. And in a moment, anger, pity, humiliation, a compound of every deep feeling of the human heart rose within me. For I saw that almost every one of those children had mis-shapen legs or ankles.

They had felt the weakening drag of malnutrition, because there was so little money coming into the mining areas at that time.

When I asked a Member of Parliament about this tragedy, he said, "Well, it's very sad. But if they spent the dole on milk for the children instead of beer for themselves, they'd be better off."

Perhaps there was some truth in the remark. I cannot say. But it sounded so cynical and it was so inadequate. It filled me with fury. I cursed God and man, especially that man. It was this feeling of disillusionment which springs up in the individual human heart at the bad moments when faith and hope are beyond the horizon, and which Lenin encouraged and integrated into a world-wide revolutionary movement. If the metallic Russian had been with me then, I should have been happy to string that M.P. up to a Whitehall lamp-post.

Yet somewhere deep in my spirit the nagging, reluctant question stirred, "Human poverty and misery are vile—but does that make it right to hang or shoot people merely because they happen to be rich?"

I believed in Justice. And by Justice, I did not mean merely Justice *for* those I liked *against* those I did not like. I meant the old democratic conception of Justice—Justice for all.

Somehow I could not believe in a Justice which decreed terrorism against a particular race or class, however much from time to time I might have liked to see it operate.

Lenin, in drafting the Soviet penal code, declared, "The legal trial is not intended to replace terrorism, but to base terrorism firmly on a fundamental principle."

I did not want Justice in the shape of terrorism based firmly on a fundamental principle. I thought terrorism was wrong.

But was my own answer right? I answered the challenge of slums, poverty, unemployment, with a fine passionate liberal spirit which I thought very noble, which hurt nobody, least of all myself, and which I hoped in time would make things better.

My own remedy for the state of affairs was twofold. First, I with violence and sincerity attacked and blamed the men in charge of the State for their bungling and indifference.

Second, I made up my mind that I would get into Parliament myself one day, and by winning power for myself put right the wrongs of the nation.

I had better chances than most for exercising those qualities of criticism coupled with personal ambition which were the best contribution so many of us were able to make to the inter-war world.

For I worked in Fleet Street. I was able to get out my views on millions of breakfast tables, day after day, week after week.

.   .   .   .   .

For seven long years I gave Fleet Street my life. In return Fleet Street gave me three F's, Fun, Fame and Fortune. It was a more ample return than is received from most things to which men devote their lives.

At nine o'clock each night those massive steel and

concrete structures in Fleet Street begin to quake and tremble like corn before the evening breeze. The very pinnacle of the roof shakes and oscillates at the moment when, embedded fifty feet below the surface of the earth, the sprawled machines begin to revolve and pour forth million upon million of newspapers to every corner of Britain until the daylight comes again.

Life in Fleet Street is a bug. It burrows beneath your skin and into your blood-stream.

There is a loyalty and a gaiety of comradeship and a zest and a stir among the Black Brotherhood of Ink. Life tastes strong and distinctive in the Street. Its flavours there are full and grip the throat.

You are of the world and in the world and yet above the world. You scan life from a crow's-nest, the waves and tides of humanity surge and struggle and break around you. You perceive the toil and triumph, the suffering and success, the tears and the tumult, the complaints and the applause. You groan and rejoice in sympathy—for every good reporter must feel in his own heart, and so understand, the emotions and the motives he describes. Yet all the time you remain a spectator and an observer. And some can still be found in Fleet Street, not enough, but a valiant section, who hold their pens unimpassioned and without bias, servants only of the truth and masters of humanity.

With it all, life in the Street can be a jungle business— the survival of the foremost and death to the hindmost. The dives and joints which surround Fleet Street are awash with those who for one reason or another have not stood their feet and have been carried off by the tide.

Journalists seldom retire, though all declare they long for the day when they will do so. Some rise to the top of their profession. Some take to drink or get fired or go into politics. But they stick to the Black Craft.

There is a sense of power in the knowledge that the words you write late at night will affect the thinking of millions of homes on the morning after. Many journalists whose names you would not recognise consider that they exercise a greater influence on public events than some well-known politicians who make speeches at by-election after by-election. The journalists are right.

How much can the fate of nations be affected by small things. More than once I have seen leader columns, potent and splenetic, which have created confusion in the Ministerial Minds and have rocked Cabinets. And in my heart I have laughed, knowing that the spleen in the leader column, the real sting of it, was due to the fact that the writer had just had a row with his lady-love or had drunk too much at luncheon and made an ass of himself.

I took a degree at Fleet Street University. I learned how the wheels go round—not the big wheels you see, but the little ones inside the machine of life which produce traction. I learned of the oil which smooths the water and of the grease which eases the pathway to success.

And that oil and grease which were so indispensable a part of the inter-war world became very much a part of my own living. As I learned the technique of back-scratching and man-pleasing which are needed for self-advancement, my fine ideals became less noticeable.

Sometimes, as I worked in Fleet Street, hungry for my articles to be praised and recognised, sore if they were abused or neglected, I remembered my childhood Sunday afternoons. I spent them in church—a regular and enforced visitation.

There was a children's service. From the pulpit the preacher asked questions which the children had to answer. "Who killed the giant Goliath?" he would ask.

Half the children were scared to answer to that white-surpliced figure which towered above them. Half the children did not know the answer. I belonged to both halves.

But the stern and be-boned elbow of my adult escort would dig me a dig. "David," the voice would whisper in my ear. Then another dig, "Go on, say David."

And obediently I would gulp and mutter "David" from our pew.

"Very good, very good," the preacher would remark from the heights above and a smile like sunrise would dawn above the surplice, while my escort would proudly look around, taking to herself the admiration of her charge. Of course I quickly lost my sense of fright at answering the preacher. For I loved the glory of praise and the warm feeling of being the centre of admiring glances. Young as I was I hungered for it. As soon as the preacher asked his questions I would eagerly listen for the prompting whisper from my right, and bawl out the answer swiftly lest anyone should beat me. I was in such a hurry to reply that one day I shouted "Abraham" when the answer should have been "Ahab".

Twenty-five years later I was in the full flush of triumph as a political writer, battering at the ramparts of achievement, and storming them one by one. Yet I often remembered that Brighton church.

Then I was invited to a City dinner, to make a speech in reply to the toast of the guests.

I had never been to a City dinner. I accepted.

A few days before the dinner I was sent the list of guests for whom I was to reply. It contained the names of some of the most successful in the land, men in whose hands the destiny of this country's government and business rested in those inter-war years. You would know those names if I set them down on paper for you.

My emotions on receiving this list were twofold. I was excited at the opportunity, but fearful of failure.

At that time I was working in close touch with Lord Beaverbrook. Most days I spent hours in his company.

Lord Beaverbrook is a man whose knowledge is clear and deep. He is a scholar of humanity. His special subject is human weakness. He knows it sideways, backwards and end to end.

I told him of the situation in which I found myself. I asked what I should say in my speech.

He sat, a small figure in a huge chair. A great grin then creased his countenance. He said, "Peter, pour the soft oil of flattery down their backs. You will find men cannot have too much of it, however much they protest they do not like it."

I wrote out a speech, including a friendly reference to each guest of distinction. It seemed high-pitched in its terms of adulation. I read it to Lord Beaverbrook.

He did not approve. His criticism was based on the fact that my references were not oily enough.

I redecorated my phrases in accordance with Lord Beaverbrook's suggestions. When the moment came at the City banquet I arose. I poured out my praises with such appearance of sincerity as I could muster. My white tie and tail coat helped to give tone to the occasion. As I sat down, the thought crossed my mind, "It's too much. Nobody could swallow that dose."

The applause was a cannonade. I was undoubtedly the success of the evening. One distinguished guest, shook my hand and said, "If I may say so, Howard, you are a very remarkable young man."

"Pour the soft oil of flattery down their backs—men cannot have too much of it." Lord Beaverbrook was right.

I knew it myself. I found my heart pounding with pleasure at the compliment which had been paid me.

As I drove home in the taxi that night, suddenly, upon my cinema-screen mind flashed a moving-picture of a small boy in a Brighton church all those years ago, with an Eton collar sawing his neck, tensely waiting the whisper from his escort, shouting the answer and looking round to catch the applause.

A week or two later I received an invitation to wear the Livery of the City Company whose guest I had been and also to become a Freeman of the City of London.

So I went up in the world. I was quick to learn the lessons of life and saw the way to get on.

Once I wrote of a Left Wing politician, "He came to London with the fires of revolution burning in his belly—but they were quenched by other men's champagne."

This, literally and figuratively, became true of myself as I went up in the world. The good things of life, as they came my way, blunted my resentment about the bad things of life which came the way of others.

Success became an end in itself, instead of a means of righting the wrongs of the world. I was a part of that complacent, man-pleasing age which spent so much time telling itself the things it wanted to hear instead of the things it ought to hear.

Part of an age when politicians withheld facts about the world situation in case it cut their party popularity.

Part of an age where newspapers poured out prosperity stories up to the very eve of the greatest explosion in human history, knowing these stories keep folk happy and are food for advertising revenue.

Chapter IV

FOOTBALL BOOTS AND SPIKES

MY grandfather was an unexpected fellow. He was both bearded and beloved. His name was Ebenezer.

When he was over eighty, I sought his advice on a certain course of action. Already I had decided to take that course, whatever advice my grandfather offered. But I hoped the old gentleman would be pleased and flattered at my enquiry. The following conversation took place between us on the platform of Bexhill West station as I waited for his train.

MYSELF: "Grandfather, there's something I want your advice about."

GRANDFATHER (fiercely): "Well, Peter, you shall have my advice, but you won't pay attention to it."

MYSELF (stung by the truth of this observation): "You see, I am wondering whether I should . . ."

GRANDFATHER: "Don't bother to tell me about it. I don't want to hear it. My advice to you and all young men is, '*Don't Do It*.' Then they usually do do it, and afterwards they are sorry."

No more would my grandfather, Ebenezer, say. He climbed puffing into the train. The train climbed puffing out of the station. I was left, punctured, on the platform.

I add, in order to confirm the elderdom and betterdom of my grandfather that I *did* do it and *was* sorry afterwards.

But the advice "Don't do it" is one ever offered by age to youth, and ever repugnant to it. The simple words "Don't do it" have incited young people to more acts of defiance and folly than any other three in the language.

My left leg was responsible for a piece of advice which altered my course. My left leg is lame. I was born with it that way. Since birth it has been little thicker than my wrist and I have never been able to point my toe.

At the age of seven I sprained this leg, playing football with my friends. The doctor who examined the sprain said to me, "Well, cricket is a better game for you. Don't play football. You stick to cricket, there's a good boy." He went away.

It was at that moment, I think, that the desire to be a footballer sprang to life inside me. As my father and Arthur, my uncle, had both been rugby footballers, rugby was the game for me.

I used as a boy to spend my shilling and sway with the mackintoshed multitude on the mound at Twickenham. Out on the green before us the team would weave the pattern of the game, miniatured by the distance, uncanny in precision and skill, resilient against injury, emblems of power and poise and purpose.

And there was the exhilaration and rough humour and warmth of a British crowd. The stamping of feet and the shouts and shuffling as the terraces began to fill. The man with a megaphone who yelled orders and packed us patiently into position, while we chaffed and cheered him in turn.

The oranges and sandwiches, the rattles and whistles and songs.

Bagpipes for the Scottish match, the green hats and streamers for Ireland, and for the Welsh "Land of My Fathers", sung by the seventy thousand so you caught your breath and your eyes filled with tears—a moment later the annual avalanche of laughter as a little Welshman ducked out on to the field and shinned up to the and moan and gabble of the multitude bursting through the window, a frightening but intoxicating sound, I discovered that I had failed to bring my puttees from England. I was determined that the England selectors should never notice on the field how thin my left leg really was in case they took fright and dropped me from the side. So I used to roll two puttees around it, mould them into the shape of a sound leg and pull my stocking over them.

Now the puttees were gone. The game was due to begin in five minutes. I ran into the washplace. I grabbed a towel from the rail, rammed it somehow around my leg and tied my stocking over it.

Off we ran on to the field. The air was blurred with the uproar of the Dublin crowd, co-mingled with the shouts of the boat-loads of English supporters who had made the night crossing to watch the game. The whistle blew.

I can see that ball now, silhouetted like a yellow lemon against the grey Dublin skies, dropping and twisting towards us. I caught it and kicked to touch as three Irishmen sprang on top of me and knocked the breath out of my bones against the grass.

It was a wearing, tearing, worrying, scurrying game. Once, breaking from the scrum, I caught the ball inside our own twenty-five line and ran up the field. Three times Irishmen tried to tackle me—three times I ran on after a stumble and stagger. Finally the full-back crashed me down only a few yards from the Irish line.

It was during the last twenty yards of the run, which sticks in my mind because it was far the longest distance I ever was allowed to carry the ball in a first-class game, that I sensed rather than saw something white snapping or worrying at my heels as I moved. I thought it might be a terrier dog escaped from the crowd.

As the full-back knocked me over, I perceived a shriller sound of merriment mixed with the deep baying of the multitude's applause. Then I noticed that the towel with which so urgently I had padded my leg was trickling behind me. I snatched it off, pretending to laugh. But I felt bitterness within me—forty thousand people, all laughing at me.

We lost the match by a single point. It was a game we should have won. There was a certain gloom and despondency in our midst that evening. Next day the newspapers with their accounts of the match arrived. I grabbed them. And I quickly saw that while the play of the England team as a whole was in a measure criticised, my own part of the performance was upheld for commendation. The word Howard was repeated many times in those newspapers.

From that moment any regret at the loss of the match disappeared from my heart. Other folk on the side stayed glum. I pretended to stay glum. Yet inwardly I glowed.

This was the first time in which I clearly recognised a fact which remained true throughout my football days. And here it is. I always would rather be the star on a losing side than blush unseen on a winning one. I was concerned more with my own glory than with the fate of my side.

I concealed this successfully from many people. Sometimes I even concealed it from myself. Indeed, at rugger dinners I constantly made speeches on the themes of "team spirit" and "the game's the thing"—and meant it while I said it.

But from the day after that Dublin match I knew deep down in my heart that my own success and fame were the things I really hunted on the rugger field. And these same motives were woven into the pattern and which war broke out, offered a fine chance for international sport to prove its healing influence. There were Germans and Italians, French, British and Americans, as well as most of the Balkan countries. We might have hoped for a period of goodwill and friendliness, in which the young men of these different nations set aside the bitterness of their rulers and united in friendship for a few days with a common love of sport. I hoped it. But it was not to be.

Instead, a warlike feeling developed which would have been comical, had it not been so hostile and tense. The whole Championship resolved itself into the question, not of who would win it, but of whether we should beat the Germans or the Germans beat us.

The American team were our strong allies. The Italians, on the other hand, cheered the Germans loudly from the grand stands and in public, and occasionally booed or whistled as the British team flashed by.

At night, in the privacy of our hotel, some of the Italians came to visit us, and begged us with tears in their eyes to beat the Germans, as they thought we were the only team likely to do so.

Constantly in my newspaper I was telling British diplomats and Foreign Secretaries how to behave. Here, at Cortina, was a chance to put my theories into practice. But when I was confronted with an international situation in miniature, I found that my contribution was to see clearly how badly the others were behaving, to disapprove of them, to feel superior and to hold myself aloof.

There were some strange interludes in this warfare. The Italians had built a wonderful racing track at Cortina. But it finished at the finishing post. They had forgotten that the bobs raced past that point at nearly one hundred miles an hour and needed at least a quarter of a mile of surfaced and uphill ice before they could pull up in safety.

The result was that the most dangerous part of the race came after you had finished the course. The Germans found themselves quite unable to take the corner after the finishing post. They crashed there almost every time. By the last day of the Championship they had been reduced by injuries from four teams to one.

They displayed a cold courage which startled and frightened us. One German team crashed badly. Two of the men were seriously injured and had to go to hospital. Another was cut on his thigh. The fourth, the captain, had a gash nearly four inches long on his cheek. As we ran forward to help, the captain picked himself up, surveyed his fallen and writhing comrades, then turned his back on them and marching to the timekeeper's hut said in German, "What was our time, please?"

The Belgians also crashed here. One of their team was injured and they had no reserve to take his place. They were doing well in the races and had one more descent to make to complete the course. That night they scoured the bars of Cortina, searching for some Belgian who would make the descent for the glory of his nation. Around midnight they found him. He was a charming, unassuming and above all unsuspicious young man who knew nothing about bobbing.

Lobsters turn from black to red very swiftly when plunged into boiling water. Humans change yet more swiftly from pink to green when plunged down an ice track on a racing bob without knowing what they are in for.

How they held him on remains a mystery. But they made good time and the young Belgian was rightly a hero of Cortina.

After the first two days we made a united and vehement

protest to the authorities about the dangerous state of the track. They went into conference and presently emerged with beaming smiles, saying, "To-morrow everything will be all right."

Next day we eagerly visited the danger point before climbing the mountain to the start. The track was as it always had been. Evidently the job of reconstruction had been too heavy to undertake.

But there was an addition to the amenities. An aged and lovable gentleman with long drooping moustaches had been stationed there. He had an open penknife in his hand. He explained that his job was to scrape the blood off the ice if there was a spill, so that the onlookers should not suffer from any feelings of distress.

We had no reserves for our British team. So we provided ourselves with drugs in case any of us suffered injury. For, injured or not, we were resolved to get the bob down the track somehow or other.

The first day of the Championships we made a bad beginning. We got the worst of the draw, having to race on a badly cut-up track after the sun had risen and a slight thaw had taken the bite and speed out of the ice. The Germans led us by over a second.

On the three following days, the situation improved. We broke the world's record for the Cortina run on each occasion, doing better every day, and finally ended ahead of the Germans.

It would be idle to pretend that this triumph gave everybody satisfaction. There was a sultry atmosphere as we moved into the hotel to receive our prizes.

Countess Ciano stood behind a table loaded with vast pots decorated with Fascist emblems. She had hoped to hand them to the Germans. Now they had come to us.

The Countess had learned one of her father's mannerisms. A friend told me she used to practise it in front of a mirror until she got it right. She was able suddenly to open her eyes so wide that a white ring showed all around the pupils. This gave her a mesmeric and demoniac gaze. She now turned it full force upon us as we sat before her waiting for our prizes.

A band was provided to play the National Anthem. Unfortunately, owing to some misunderstanding or more probably because our victory over the Germans had upset previous arrangements, when the words "Great Britain" were shouted and we advanced towards the Countess to collect our pots, the band broke into a loud and spirited rendering of "Deutschland über Alles."

The Germans looked furious. We stood to attention with British phlegm. But the Countess, after giving the band a glance almost loud enough to drown their music, suddenly burst into peals of shrill laughter.

Then she gave us our pots and we took our departure. We had a happy party with the American team that evening. We talked together of the Olympic Games which were to be held at the end of that fateful year, 1939, in Germany at Garmisch and at which some of us had been invited to represent our nations.

Next day we went our several ways. Some blood had been shed and some bad blood created by the World's Bobsleigh Championship at Cortina. That was the main result of it all.

I returned to England with my pot. I shut it in a cupboard, where it has stayed ever since.

I was out for other trophies from life, and I did not have to travel so far afield as Cortina to lay my hands upon them.

CHAPTER V

LORD BEAVERBROOK BREAKS A HORSE

SUCCESS was my aim. I sought it through power. And I sought it through money.

I lived to manhood at a time when most young men like myself believed that our first duty to ourselves, our families and our nation was to get ourselves along in the world. But did we get the world along? I, for one, never stopped to think what sort of nation would be produced by millions of individuals all selfishly elbowing, manœuvring and tearing each other's throats to obtain for themselves a larger cut off the national joint.

In the poem, the old farmer gives his son this advice, "I don't say marry for money—but go where the money is." I went where the money was. I worked for Lord Beaverbrook in Fleet Street.

Lord Beaverbrook has an eye like a harpoon.

It transfixes and imprisons. Once at a dinner party I felt as it were a stab in my blubber and, turning, saw that I was hooked and held in this whale-wise manner. "Peter," said Beaverbrook, "you should write some paragraphs for the *Evening Standard* on the subject of accents —the way in which different men pronounce different words. Lord Curzon for example—the late and great, I mean. He always used to pronounce the word 'dance' as though it rhymed with 'pants'. Then you might say Lord Beaverbrook always calls the horse race the DURBY except when he remembers to call it the DARBY."

At this point a friend of Lord Beaverbrook's, a woman of intelligence and courage, remarked, "Peter, you will be nearer the truth if you say Max always calls it the DARBY except when he remembers to call it the DURBY."

Lord Beaverbrook's Canadian accent is something which he cherishes. He takes pains to retain it, after more than thirty years of life in England.

Indeed his Canadian accent is so fetching that it is catching. And this imitation gives him much delight, coupled with a secret and cynical amusement.

Lord Beaverbrook had a friend. His name was Rudyard Kipling. Lord Beaverbrook, studying and admiring the art of his friend, decided that he himself must learn to write stout and active prose.

Lord Beaverbrook in early life was a chemist's assistant. He still delights to call for a bottle and to demonstrate to the astonished guests how he can hold it round the waist and at the same time with the same hand pluck the cork from its neck. By the age of twenty-five he had carved an immense fortune. He crossed the Atlantic to a strange land, entered Parliament, became the instrument to kill a government which seemed at that time imperishable and to establish Lloyd George's war-winning administration.

Then he became a baron.

And it is a sign of Lord Beaverbrook's strength and balance that with all his achievement and ability he was not too proud to go back to school again.

He sat doggedly under Rudyard Kipling. From this friend, with resolution, he learned to think in ink—to write prose. His style to-day is an artificial one. But forthright and distinctive.

Like his accent, it is catching.

One Thursday evening Lord Beaverbrook, a man whose hand I once had shaken, telephoned to me at the solicitor's office where then I worked. He asked me to go and see him. As soon as I got inside the room, he said, "I want you to write a political article for me."

This was the first I knew of the proposition. Just the

But at the end of seven years of this sort of process, you become in the words of the song "A Little Bit Independent", just a little bit immunised, like the Roman Emperors, against both kinds of drug. The old limbs do not jerk so instantly into action at the blame nor do they put on so heart-wrenching a spurt at the praise.

And all that memory leaves behind is a sense of affection and gratitude. By and large it was more fun than fury.

During those seven years my objective was to please my boss. It would be foolish to deny that I succeeded. During the seven years I worked with him, my salary was multiplied by six.

Money, money, money—the great God £. s. d. I worked, schemed and fought for it. I was one of a mighty inter-war army of British citizens who spent the greater part of their lives struggling by kicks or kisses to extract a rise in pay from their employers.

I was so set on pleasing my boss that I did not greatly care whether I displeased some others in the process —provided those I displeased had nothing to offer me, and could do me no harm.

Sometimes my hot anger against conditions flared up in genuine resentment against our public men.

I had seen so much misery and poverty in our midst while the fat and the rich still flourished. Some public men made fine speeches on public platforms, but when I met them in private, they seemed ineffective, complacent and even indifferent. I yearned and strove to scald them into action.

Being myself by nature extremely sensitive to criticism, I was able to diagnose to the millimetre the most tender spots in the anatomy of other people. Some of them used to yelp to Lord Beaverbrook for sympathy. If they were of sufficient importance, he would give them their sympathy—and give me a rise in pay.

So my resentment against our politicians paid dividends.

Sometimes the newspaper's policy had to be advocated by folk like myself, even if I did not wholly endorse it. But my highly-paid job meant more to me than my scruples.

I signed my name to many views which I at most but half believed.

I suppose in my seven years of political and leader writing, I told more people what to do or what to stop doing than any other political journalist.

I made a name and I made money for myself. That was my aim and my achievement.

Yet I cannot recall any man of power who, to suit my written observations, modified or changed his conduct by a particle.

I had no answer for the man of power. And, to be frank, the men of power had no answer for me. They gave no leadership of the quality to match the age. They left me either hot with rage or cold with indifference.

Their lives, on the whole, seemed to be based on the same motives of personal ambition as my own, while the cures they propounded for the ills of the nation were based on the belief that more money for somebody would put everything right.

That was my belief, and I was the somebody.

As I and my generation tried with varying success to carve out a position in life, the shadows were lengthening across Europe. On the Continent young men with clubs and castor oil, with Gestapo and Ogpu, with purges and liquidations were smashing aside every human barrier which stood between them and the fulfilment of their big ideas.

I and millions like me in Britain had our own ideas. Many of them were, on the whole, well-meaning and well-intended. But above all we wanted to be left alone, to be allowed to get on with our job of getting on.

For a long time we hoped we could answer tanks by talk, disruption by disapproval, and passion by penmanship.

Some of the things I and my generation believed in were the good and the right things. But being right is both smug and inadequate in a world where those whose idea it is to establish wrong are on the march.

What I and my generation never learned was how to establish right. We did not understand how to make What Is Right the strongest idea in the world.

We never faced or paid the cost of making ideals effective. Some of us thought we could couple the theory of high ideals with the practice of low living.

So the idea of democracy, which is the name we in Britain gave to our idea, became debased. It lost the character of true democracy. It surrendered the initiative to those forces in the world which worked and lived for the spreading of their anti-democratic ideas among all nations by means of force and revolution.

As a nation, we lightly skipped over our own mistakes while urging other nations, by means of pious pronouncements, to become different. This method has never influenced me when it has been applied to me. Nor did it influence the other nations.

Meanwhile I and millions like me continued to disapprove of much that went on but failed to do anything effective about it. We booed from the back seat while the world charabanc was driven over the precipice by those who desired a crash.

Chapter VI

I SPY STRANGERS

IN my early Fleet Street days I learned the story of the first Parliamentary gossip-columnist, who got a scoop which has made history. He was a junior official of the House of Commons. He was on duty on January 4, 1642. That is the last occasion a British King entered the Chamber of the House of Commons.

On that day Charles I came down with an armed guard to arrest five Members of Parliament who had offended him. The junior official had been forbidden to write about anything which went on in Parliament. But he kept under cover and took a shorthand note of all that was said on that memorable occasion.

So we have the story.

King Charles strode in. He demanded to be told where the Five Members were. Nobody answered.

Actually the Five Members had been tipped off by a lady. They had escaped in a boat across the Thames a few moments before the King arrived at Westminster. Charles then addressed Lenthall, the Speaker, and ordered him to hand the culprits over.

Lenthall went on his knees, but refused to give any information, saying that he had neither eyes, nor ears, nor mouth, save with the permission of the House of Commons.

So, at the risk of life itself (and indeed at the cost of much bloodshed, for the Civil War followed quickly after these incidents), Parliament established the sovereignty of the people, against Kings, dictators or anyone at all, inside or outside their ranks, who would exert tyranny.

To this day, when the Gentleman Usher of the Black Rod arrives at the House of Commons bidding them attend the King in the House of Lords, the door is slammed in his face. He has to knock three times before he is allowed inside to deliver his message.

To this day, when a new Speaker is elected, he has to be dragged forcibly to the Chair and held there—relic of the days of men like Speaker Lenthall, when all were reluctant to assume an office which involved the risks of defying in the name of the people the most powerful men of the nation.

To this day a carpet divides the two sides of the House of Commons, a carpet too wide for swords to meet across it. Those who speak in Parliament must not step over the edge of the carpet—relic of the days when Parliament pioneered the democratic tradition of free speech coupled with good humour.

What warmth and colour and majesty are woven into the story of Parliament.

Here Burke pleaded, gloriously but in vain, for justice to the American colonists.

Here Pitt, unmoved by crisis or catastrophe, held Britain to the task of saving herself by her exertions and Europe by her example.

Here Wilberforce fought his battle for the slaves against every obstruction of calumny, prejudice and entrenched self-interest.

Here Disraeli risked his career to plead for tolerance towards his own great race, the Jews.

Here Gladstone offered moral and spiritual leadership to his age.

And here, in more recent times, Churchill radiated a dauntless spirit of unconquerable resolve through the darkest stages of our journey.

In the inter-war years I longed, like many young men,

to get into Parliament, to take my place and play my part in that great pageant of the people.

Apart from this, I thought it would be another step up the ladder of success as well as offering another string to my journalistic bow. Also, I thought I could do better than most of the folk who were inside there.

In those days my Tory convictions were much to the fore. When a vacancy occurred in a certain Parliamentary division, I put on my best coat and went to see the Chairman.

I told him I would like to be a candidate.

He informed me I was just the sort of fellow they were looking for. Then he asked, "How much will you subscribe to the local association?" I answered that I did not wish to make money out of public life, but would give my Parliamentary salary.

He replied, "I am sorry, Mr. Howard. We have already been offered £1,000 a year. If you can't do better than that, I'm afraid it is out of the question."

This was my first introduction to the power of money in the British democratic system. But I soon discovered that many good Tory seats were up for sale.

On the Labour side also, a seat in Parliament was sometimes awarded, almost in the nature of an honourable pension and retirement, to those who had grown old in Trade Union service.

Of course, if I had got into Parliament, I should have been out for a job in the Government—and a title too, if it came my way. So I was not surprised to discover that many Members of Parliament were out for those very things.

During the first Great War against Germany, there was a fierce and close Parliamentary division. The Government, of which Lord Birkenhead was a member, just carried the day. In the Lobby afterwards, one of Lord

Birkenhead's political opponents observed to him bitterly, "You would have been beaten but for your paid members." By "paid members" he meant all who had Government jobs or enjoyed some form of patronage from the Crown.

"Well," replied Birkenhead with urbanity, "we will give you all our paid members, if you will give us all yours who wish to be paid."

The picture is exact. Many Members of Parliament were in there for motives of personal ambition of one kind or another, and I should have swelled their ranks.

Parliament was rightly regarded by many as the sanest, soundest and strongest form of government so far devised by man. After all, it has withstood the shock of the two greatest wars in human history.

Sometimes in the inter-war years that assembly rose to great heights of dignity and effectiveness.

When you scanned the ranks of the best type of Parliamentarian, you saw what Parliament could and should be. For there were in Parliament many men of all parties who steadfastly and selflessly gave of their best, without fear or favour, in the public service. They came to Westminster with a single idea—the welfare of the nation. If all were like them, Parliament would become the Mother of Parliaments again, instead of watching the world turn away, country by country, from the democracy she pioneered.

However, it is a sad quality of human nature that if a man enjoys a first-rate dinner, but has the soup spilt down his neck, that is the part he remembers. So it was that the bad motives and conduct of some legislators coloured the public impressions of the House of Commons. People became cynical, weary and even contemptuous about politicians, and the whole institution of Parliament, although praised by many lips, kindled no fire in the hearts of the millions.

And this bad side of the penny was the one most constantly exploited and exposed by publicists like myself. Strange but true, it is easier to be controversial than constructive.

I kicked and cursed the politicians. I became bitter and black about them. Yet, looking back on those inter-war years, I believe I had the Parliament I deserved and that, by and large, the majority of the nation were given the politics they desired.

Like many millions of us, I was out for Number One first. So were a number of M.P.s. And if Howard had been multiplied six hundred and fifteen times over, and so constituted a new House of Commons, I have an unpleasant feeling that few people would have noticed any major change in our legislature.

As for policy, I and the rest of the nation wanted comfort above everything else. We wanted to be left alone.

We wanted to build arms against the dictators—but not at any personal cost.

We wanted all our rights, but forgot some of our duties.

We wanted to stop Hitler—but not if it meant sacrificing our ease and wealth to do it.

One feature of the life of our politicians and public men surprised me as I moved among them in the course of my newspaper duties, ever battering my way forward in the world. I had believed that all public men had to lead godly, righteous and sober private lives, as otherwise the public would cease to support and follow them.

I found this was not so. It was an out-of-date theory. Many of our public men, some in positions of high responsibility, were unable to say *No* to a drink, a smoke or a woman.

Divorce and adultery were not uncommon in our public life.

This discovery affected me. Ambition to get on in the world had acted as a restraint on some of my conduct. I would not do those things which I felt could damage my career.

But when I found some of our national leaders doing as they pleased, and nobody caring much about it, I began to take a more lenient view of these matters for myself.

I never perceived that leadership which was drunk with alcohol, sex, money or personal ambition could offer no answer to the leaderships drunk with power which were bidding to control the lives of millions in Europe and in Asia.

Indeed, both the Parliamentarians who allowed themselves such latitude and publicists like me who criticised and copied them played into the hands of that leadership. We pandered to those who made it their business to hold up Parliament and its members to ridicule and contempt, knowing that Parliament, with all the faults of any human institution, is our one enduring bulwark against tyranny.

CHAPTER VII

FAREWELL, MY HEART

I AND my generation in Britain were not captured by the big ideas of Hitler or Lenin, though we had no passion strong enough to outmatch their passions. Yet there was one idea, one way of life, which fascinated and allured us.

As I grew up and forced my way onward in the world, as my income and reputation increased, I became interested in the ideas put forward by men like Bertrand Russell and others, which were looked upon as "modern" and "progressive".

Briefly, men like these and the school of life they represented taught me that I ought to do as I pleased. If I denied myself greater latitude in sexual matters, for example, I was apparently suffering from things called "inhibitions", "complexes" and so forth.

Quite apart from the more serious advocacy of men like Russell, there was a glut of "modern" novels by lesser-known luminaries. I read many of these. The supreme moments in most of them gave accounts of what I always had regarded as illicit delight. Happiness was found, they declared, when people chose the sleeping partners they fancied and refused to be shackled by any foolish prejudice in favour of commitments already undertaken.

It is true that when I met the authors of these novels in the flesh they themselves seemed far from happy—gross, haggard or bitter, torn by an endless search for something just within sight yet never within reach. But men accepted their theories without bothering too much about the practice, just as they pay half a crown to

a seedy individual on a racecourse in return for a tip on
how to get rich quick.

An old friend of mine, a man who at present holds a
position of great responsibility in our national life, gave
me this advice: "Peter, if you want to get on in the
world, cut down on the drink and go in for the women."
And while plenty of my friends neglected the first half
of his advice, most of them adopted the second.

I looked around at public life, at the world of big
business, at the B.B.C., at Fleet Street. Many of the
most successful people I knew seemed to be living this
modern way.

The privileged position held by the marriage contract
in law at that time was ridiculed and attacked. The
number of divorces in Britain has more than doubled.
It was the trend of our inter-war age. Pictures were
given of an era in which life would be one prolonged and
organised act of promiscuous love while chemical babies
were produced synthetically to shape, colour, specifica-
tion and order from laboratories.

This sort of idea about sex was duplicated in European
countries where promiscuity and illegitimacy were
encouraged for the sake of the birthrate.

In Hitler's Germany the *Deutsche Textil Arbeiter* declared, "We esteem every girl who defies outmoded
conventions and justifies herself in her child born out of
wedlock." While Professor Ernst Bergman said, "Fortunately one boy of good race suffices for twenty girls and
the girls would gladly fulfil this demand were it not for
the nonsensical so-called civilised idea of monogamous
permanent marriage."

It was the same sort of system as in Lenin's land where,
at one stage of Soviet development, a law was passed
decreeing that one partner could divorce the other merely
by sending a postcard saying he no longer desired to

live with her, and where Madame Simonovitch wrote in *Pravda*, "Our young people have certain principles. And those are governed by the belief that the nearer you approach the extreme and, as it were, the animal primitiveness in matters of sexual passions, the more Communistic you are."

Back to the jungle in the name of progress. In that era Soviet Ambassadress A. Kollontai remarked, "Immorality in the schools is making satisfactory progress."

This "modern" idea that sex was merely a source of enjoyment and not a matter for restraint, won my intellectual assent as I looked around me.

Some of my friends were extreme in political affiliation. They included free love in their conception of freedom. They mocked at the old idea of "what God has joined together, let no man put asunder." They called this "bourgeois morality."

I was quite sure from the way they said it, that if there were one thing I did not wish to be it was "bourgeois", though I was not at the time quite certain what the word meant. Anyhow, I wanted to be assured that romance, in the shape which I desired it, was the correct thing, and that the scruples I felt deep down in my heart were foolish and of small importance. My extremist friends told me that my scruples were wrong and my desires were right. So naturally I became very attracted to this extremist political programme.

True my daring in romance did not match my desires. My courage was never adequate to let me live out my convictions. But I was convinced that the most sensible and intelligent people refused to be bound by the established Christian conception of morality.

Then, suddenly, real love came into my life. For me, as for thousands of other men of my generation, it brushed aside these "modern" ideas and restored in my heart the "old-fashioned" desire to marry the woman I loved and live faithfully with her.

.   .   .   .   .

The story of my romance began with a man who spent many hours of his childhood crouched inside a bread oven.

Metaxa is his name.   He is a Greek.

His mother once hid him in the oven saying pirates might come to the island of Ithaca where he was born. For pirates used to shanghai small boys from Ithaca, carry them off as cabin-hands and cook-boys on expeditions of smuggling and violence.

So one of John Metaxa's first recollections is of his mother's pale hands fluttering like moths towards him through the darkness of the oven, thrusting forward a cup of sweet wine and a hunk of bread stuffed with black olives, and swiftly withdrawing.

Metaxa ran barefoot on Ithaca.   His body grew strong and hard.   He plunged it in the bay of Ithaca, where on calm days, fathoms deep, they say you still can see pinnacles and fluted pillars of age-old palaces drowned in the ageless ocean.

John Metaxa was bred to responsibility and vision. For his family is one of the oldest in Greece.

He has a daughter.   Doris is her name, and her friends call her Doë.   My eyes first saw her in Switzerland, and my heart told me to walk and talk with her also.

She was a famous person.   She was one of the great lawn tennis players of the day.   Few women could prevail against the violence of her forehand drive, and most men were endangered by it.   It was a surprise and shock to me when first I saw the force and fury generated by so slight a person.   I felt something of the wonder which would fill the mind of the onlooker if he saw a gazelle kicking buffaloes to extinction.

A friend introduced me to Doë. So I soon discovered that to walk and talk with John Metaxa's daughter was not so ready an affair as to become familiar with some of my English friends. No appointment with the daughter could be made without sanction of the sire.

I used to telephone to the hotel at San Moritz where the Metaxas were staying. "Would it be possible for Mr. Howard to see Mlle. Metaxa this afternoon?"

Presently the concierge would bring a message, "Mademoiselle would be happy to walk at two-thirty."

At two-thirty I would go to the hotel. There would be Doë. And there would be John Metaxa too, with walking-stick, neat clothes, and the kindly but penetrating gaze of an eagle.

Doë and I would walk in front. Behind, like the detective who protects royalty, never within earshot, ever within eyeshot, ever detached, never removed, strode John Metaxa.

He was at that time over seventy. It was hot weather, the dry, parching heat of an Alpine summer. I tried to walk faster than he did to leave him far behind. But I never succeeded. He always looked cool and faintly amused as we said good-bye, while I always was sweating and faintly uncomfortable.

The man who had spent his youth on the precipitous goat-tracks of Ithaca found the tourist tracks of San Moritz very small beer by comparison.

It would be hypocrisy to pretend that I enjoyed his manœuvres. But I conceived an admiration and affection for his character.

The Metaxas went to Paris. I was back in London, living hard and paying off Oxford debts.

I wanted to see more of Doë. So I used to take a third class week-end return ticket to Paris from London. I believe in those days it cost about thirty shillings. On

Saturday night I would leave St. Pancras, travel by train to Tilbury and embark for Dunkirk. The third class accommodation on those boats was adequate but elementary. I spent most of the night on deck. I would arrive at Paris about eight o'clock on Sunday morning.

Then there was the business of getting to see Doë. She knew I was coming to Paris. Her father did not.

I used to telephone to their hotel from the Restaurant Griffon where the proprietor loved romance even to the extent of once cashing a cheque for me.

"Mr. Howard finds himself in Paris for the day. Could he call and see Mademoiselle Metaxa?" The answer would be, "Will Mr. Howard take luncheon with the family Metaxa at one o'clock?"

So I wandered around Paris on those Sunday mornings, unknown and knowing nobody. I used to drink a glass of Dubonnet, watch the anglers in the Seine, stroll and follow the pigeons and children in the Louvre gardens— and at one o'clock I would go to the Hotel Napoléon.

There would be a family lunch. I would grab a few sentences with Doë. Then good-bye again.

In the afternoon, a solitary cinema, often incomprehensible, for I did not speak French in those days. Then back to the dear, drear Gare du Nord with its odour of fresh coffee and stale garlic, trains and drains and the prickling, tangy smell which is France. Away again on the night journey to Dunkirk and Tilbury, and to my office at Westminster by nine on Monday morning.

One day I sat opposite John Metaxa of Ithaca in the Hotel Napoléon, and asked permission to marry his daughter. I told him I loved Doë. I told him I was, as far as I knew, healthy, but certainly not wealthy. I told him the things which I imagine most young men, in the nervous condition of love, do blurt out to prospective fathers-in-law.

John Metaxa said nothing. Nothing at all. I suppose we sat for two minutes looking at each other. Then he stood up and remarked, "Mr. Howard, I understand one thing—that you are a gentleman." He shook my hand. The interview ended.

To this day I have never comprehended the reason or purpose of that remark of John Metaxa to me. I can only say that from that moment he has shown to me a generosity and a love which could not be exceeded if I were his own son.

Since then I have done many things with him, and enjoy all the more in his company. He adds vigour and life to any theatrical piece. For he has a suspicion and contempt for scenes of softness and sentimentality on the stage. As the hero makes love to the heroine, you hear a crescendo of groans from John Metaxa. He interpolates the dialogue with the sound which is variously spelt as "Tut" or "Tchchah." A gentle hiss or even a whistle has also been known to leave him.

If, on the other hand, a scene pleases him, he will stand erect in his place, set his chin and shoulders square and clap his hands high in the air with determination, while he looks around with a gaze which impels others to share his emotions.

I have seen a London audience roused from apathy to enthusiasm by John Metaxa. Also I have seen a London audience break into loud laughter at the wrong moment on account of Metaxa's groans and grimaces.

He is a stern parent. When Doë plays tennis at Wimbledon, John Metaxa sits on the sideline. He carries sugar, and slips lumps of it into her hand to regale her.

Once Doë knew that her father planned to return to France with her on the day she got knocked out of the Wimbledon tournament. He was anxious to attend to some business in Marseilles. Doë was eager to stay in England as long as possible.

During the first round of the championship, when Doë had a match point against her, John Metaxa on the sideline produced a telegram form and, in the full view of Doë, who knew what he was doing, began to draft a message to his wife in France saying that he and Doë would cross the Channel that night.

Doë won that match. She won the finals of the event at Wimbledon that year and possesses the gold medal of a Wimbledon winner.

Perhaps, besides being a shrewd parent, John Metaxa is also a psychologist. He always laughs as if he felt he had some part in that victory. Certainly, he knows Doë from the arch of her skull to the arch of her feet.

Doë's character, which is so big a part of this story of adventure, is fully displayed on the tennis court. I remember one match in particular. Doë was playing an opponent of front rank. She led five games to four and forty-love.

Her opponent was serving. The first service Doë hit with terrific force a foot beyond the base-line. Fifteen-forty.

The second she hit even harder, and it landed about three inches beyond the base-line. Thirty-forty.

The third? She hit it as hard as ever I have seen a tennis ball hit. The ball looked elliptical as it travelled. The chalk flew up in a cloud from the corner where it landed, a perfect winner.

But the linesman called it "Out". The umpire questioned him. Doë's opponent told the umpire it was in. But the linesman remained obdurate. So deuce was called.

Doë lost that game.

But she won the set and the match. That is the point of the story.

Some people sail more strongly and steadily the harder the harsh winds blow. Doë is a warrior. She has the steely quality of the undaunted. If you have never seen her in difficulty or danger, you do not fully know her.

I have seen her in both, as I will tell.

She has vividness coupled with warmth. And that is an exceedingly rare combination.

. . . .

I have been five times wed. Five times to the altar in a thirty-six year span of living.

It is only fair to add for the delusion of the wise and the confusion of the ignorant that each time it was the same girl who plodded with me through the ceremonies. So we can stake out a claim, which is unique within my experience, to be a quintuple couple, five times a husband and five times a wife.

Doë and I finished this steeplechase of a marriage twelve years ago at Marseilles—once at the English church there, twice and at great length at the Greek church, once at the English Consulate, and again at the French Mairie.

I was so gay on the morning of the first day that I bowled sous down the gutter of the Rue St. Jacques and the little French children screamed and fought for them.

The French Maire had a tricolour scarf so tightly reefed about his middle that his flesh swelled out top and bottom of it like twin waves of the ocean with a trough between.

His stomach bulged with each breath. It was a poignant spectacle, and the onlookers gasped and sweated in sympathy. He took eight and a half minutes to marry us. Then he got up steam and steered towards me to kiss my cheeks. He would have done so had I not, with English pride, outsailed him.

At the Greek church an unseen choir chanted from a gallery overhead. Young girls moved before us scattering rosebuds and living orange blossoms at our feet, as thrice in a holy ritual we followed the bearded priests around the sanctuary. Over each head, Doë's and mine, a crown of wrought and delicate gold was held by friends —held at arm's length for ninety minutes without pause or respite.

At the English church, where on the afternoon of the third day the ceremonies came to an end, I had lost all nervousness. By then getting married was to me a commonplace and indeed an everyday affair. I sang "The Campbells are coming, Tra la, tra la" in an undertone to my best man as Doë and her father came up the aisle.

We spent two days getting to England. That was our honeymoon. I remember the pigeons, living and rotund, on the street by the Concorde gardens in Paris, and the thrushes, dead and roast, on the spit in the café at Avignon. We ate them with thick black gravy and thick red wine.

Arrival in England was an ordeal for Doë. Her life had been in France and her friends in England few.

My mother wept when I left England before marriage. Doë's mother wept when she left France after marriage.

It was with this salty background that Doë and I strode across the gangway on to the shore at Dover to savour the tang of life.

The stars were tender to us and the earth was warm. Doë and I were deeply in love and have remained so to this day.

Presently we discovered Doë was going to have a baby. It is the point in the married journey which so many novelists have employed their art to gild and adorn.

What were my emotions? I was astonished. There

is a feeling of wonder when the things you have often heard about happen to you.

But coupled with my feeling of astonishment was one of irritation and a tiny fear. The chief effect of the tidings was to give me a sense of impatience that something had now occurred which was beyond my control.

Doë and I were happy as we were. The birth of a child to Doë would multiply our financial commitments and other responsibilities, while in a measure subtracting from our pleasures, liberties and comforts. Marriage was, to me at least, an instrument of delight and satisfaction. The duties attached were a liability and something as swiftly as possible to be forgotten.

I wanted our child to be a boy. But I was anxious to spare Doë any disappointment on my behalf should a girl be born to us. So I kept on informing her that I was indifferent about the matter—but that on the whole I should rather like a girl.

I set down this episode on paper because it was not the first lie, but I believe the first married lie I ever told to Doë. It had a fecund family. For as the years advanced I developed a technique of "white lies" to grease the smooth descent of the matrimonial chariot.

This is the way it went. I had two clear pictures on the wall of my heart. One was of the sort of man Doë expected and believed me to be. The other of the sort of man I wanted Doë and my family to think me. Both pictures were handsome and gay—and not unlike each other.

But alas. The sad part of the affair was this. Neither picture bore any accurate resemblance to the sort of man I was.

I began to wear a mask in the home. It was only a little mask, I told myself—but it was a thick one. I would recount to Doë my successes in journalism. I would pass on the conversations with my employer, Lord Beaverbrook, or other men of power at which my own achievements were commended. But if I received a kick or a curse, as do those who work in offices and certainly in newspaper offices, I became an oyster. I clamped my lips and said nothing. And I told myself this was to spare Doë anxiety, though, incidentally, my own pride was cushioned by these tactics.

Now I was in love with Doë. I remained in love with her. I have stayed so since we met. Yet, quite soon after our marriage, I discovered to my surprise that my interest in the freshness of lips, soft eyes and the beauty and admiration of other women had not left me. My interest was academic. But the margin between an academic interest and an actual interest was like hair on a bald man's head. It diminished slowly but steadily with the years.

My old ideas that the conception of married fidelity was bourgeois, returned to me.

I told myself that there was little harm in what I did so long as Doë had no cause for grief. If she knew nothing, she could not feel sad on that account.

In fact, as my married journey ran on, I found that the ideas propagated by gentlemen like Bertrand Russell were deep-rooted in my heart and desire. They had been covered up rather than cured by happy marriage.

Sometimes I took an evening off from the home. I worked hard to earn money for it. And I felt that a man who worked hard was entitled to his relaxations, wherever they might lie. So now and again, when I could have gone home, I would spend time dancing and drinking with the West End lassies and lads who shimmered and glimmered the hours and years away in the inter-war period.

Doë thought, or at least was told, that I was on newspaper work on such occasions. And indeed I did pick up gossip this way around the town.

Naturally the following evening I would return home early, often bringing some small gift to Doë. I would devote myself entirely to her. We would go out together, perhaps to some cavernous café in Soho to eat pungent-spiced continental dishes, to hear French talked and talk it together, to rejoice in the fun of each other's company. These were the best evenings of life. I found it hard to see while they lasted how I could ever want to spend them differently. And yet, and yet.

So our marriage ran, Doë's and mine—a gay and rippling journey, like a Dartmoor stream, with light and shade, the sudden sharp and jagged rock, the occasional calm, still stretch of deeper water.

And presently, before you can see why or how, the waters are divided—two streams run side by side where one travelled the heather before—the waters still chatter and laugh and run together for a time and then perhaps in different directions. In their shrunken and divided condition they tinkle still but lose the deeper notes.

Doë and I found each had corners in our lives which belonged to ourselves alone and not to each other. We felt that normal. We found it the way to live. A wife has the right to her own friends. A man must have some privacy. That is what we told each other, with a spontaneity of the lips and a sadness of the heart.

Two more children were born to us, a girl, Anne, and another boy, Anthony. I became what men call a Success. I sweated up the cold lower slopes of the mountain of achievement, so full of crevasses and ice and the sudden precipitous fall beneath the seeming-solid surface. I began to climb steadily and with self-satisfaction and new confidence on the sunlit upper slopes towards the ever-distant summit of my ambition.

Meanwhile Philip, our eldest son, grew up. He was four—then five—then six. And one day I looked at my son across the table of our home and I knew he was a stranger. He too had his privacy which neither I nor Doë could share. He had secrets he would not tell.

I remember the incident of the apple—so small a thing, and yet so immense to us. In a small home, if someone takes a bite out of an apple on a plate, the grown-ups usually have an idea who that someone is. "Philip," said Doë, "did you bite that apple?"

"No, Mummy, I didn't," said Philip, those brown eyes scanning us both with so direct a gaze of determination and defiance, the look I often had seen staring back at me from the mirror as I shaved in the mornings and threw over my shoulder to Doë my own account of the occupations of the evening before.

Philip told us a lie about the apple. We knew it was a lie. He knew it was a lie. It was the first time Philip ever put on his mask in our home. How to deal with it? Neither Doë nor I had the smallest idea. We told each other that it was the natural thing for children to lie to their parents in that sort of way. We remembered lies we ourselves had told in childhood.

But I had things which seemed of more importance and interest to me than the question of Philip's lie about the apple. I might not have any answer to that but I had the ear of millions for my political pronouncements.

And with a sigh of relief, I made my way to Fleet Street, brooding over the form and savouring the phrases which I should use to scald the tail of some statesman who had deceived the public, or to denounce a falsehood uttered by one of the latter-day revolutionaries of Europe.

CHAPTER VIII

MR. CHURCHILL SHARPENS HIS SWORD

FAR underground, below the granite pavements and wood-block roadways of Ludgate Circus, the river Fleet takes its secret journey to the Thames. Its waters are black as the ink of the street which takes its name.

No fish are found to-day in the river Fleet. But plenty exercise their fins and flippers in the torrents and pools of Fleet Street. Most of them are sprats or sharks, though a few genuine whales stir the depths of the waters from time to time.

One of the whales during my days in Fleet Street was Winston Churchill. For some time he worked as a colleague of mine on Lord Beaverbrook's *Evening Standard*.

He did not take such pains over his articles as he has always taken over his speeches. For many years, Churchill wrote out every word of his Parliamentary speeches in his own handwriting. Then he used to boom away at a looking-glass in the privacy of his bedroom, rehearsing them till he got each word perfect, including most of the "impromptus" which still adorn a Churchill oration.

At this stage in his career, Churchill was down on his luck politically. His newspaper articles were, in a sense, potboilers. True, they were the best things of their kind appearing at the time, but not always of the supreme literary quality which is Churchill at his best.

The Prime Minister-to-be used to read my political articles with care though not always with appreciation. He helped me greatly with comments and suggestions which found their way to me

He took exception to the phrase "For why?" which I used from time to time. He would steam up to me in the Lobby of the House of Commons, looking like a formidable battleship pouting "For why? For why?" at me aggressively through the funnel of his mouth.

In those days Churchill was a man possessed by one big idea.

Hitler's big idea was "One race shall rule."

Lenin's big idea was "One class shall rule."

Churchill's big idea was "The Nazis shall not rule. They must be destroyed." This was not a popular idea in Britain. For those were the days when the British public's desire for peace outmatched their desire to beat down Hitler. Both the British public and Churchill knew that his big idea could only be achieved by war.

Churchill had no substantial backing in his own party. He had the active distrust and hostility of the Labour Party and of the Leftists. Many remembered his part in breaking the General Strike and his editorship of *The British Gazette*. Some others recalled the days when our future true-Blue Premier had spoken with candour, expansiveness and exuberance of our future Red allies.

So Churchill sat all by himself in the moonlight, or almost, it seemed, in the sunset of a career which had somehow missed greatness. His war-song against the Nazis was almost a solo. Just the same he sang it fortissimo in the columns of the *Evening Standard*.

Meanwhile my boss, Lord Beaverbrook, the proprietor of that newspaper, was advocating the cause of Splendid Isolation. He was coining phrases such as "There will be no war this year or next year either." He was paying me a large salary to write leaders on the subject. And he was entirely opposed to Mr. Churchill's big idea.

So Percy Cudlipp, then editor of the *Evening Standard*, experienced something of the sensations of a football during a Cup Final. Fortunately Percy has toughness, resilience and a sense of humour, which are qualities needed by any successful football.

His phone would ring in the morning, "Cudlipp? This is Lord Beaverbrook here. What's the name of that fellow who writes in your paper? . . . What's his name? . . . Yes, Winston Churchill, that's the fellow I mean. Now, Percy, I hope you're not paying him too much for his articles? . . . Good God, all that? You don't mean it. That's terrible, terrible. . . . Well, anyway, I hope you're not tied up too long with him— how long does his contract run? . . . Good God, a year? Another whole year? Well now, see here, Percy, get him off the subject of the Nazis. He's obsessed by this damned fellow Hitler. Get him on to the Broad Home Theme, the great themes of the Empire, Unemployment, Agriculture—let him write on subjects like that. Anything else? Good-bye to you."

And Percy would find the telephone dead in his hand. Then he would ring up Mr. Churchill. The conversation would run something like this.

"Good morning, Mr. Churchill. What will your article be about this week?"

"Good morning, Mr. Cudlipp. I thought we should deal this week with the subject of the Nazis. We must awaken the country to the danger of this gang of criminals, and I feel we could profitably discuss the Nazi dreams of expansion in the Balkans this week."

"Yes, Mr. Churchill, that would be most interesting. But I wonder if perhaps this week an article on the Broad Home Theme might give our readers a change—some subject like Unemployment or Agriculture?"

"Quite so, Mr. Cudlipp, quite so. And we *will* come on to the Broad Home Theme. But I think *this* week a strong declaration on the Nazis will be more timely."

c

And the telephone would again go silent.

One evening I had to go to Churchill's country home on newspaper business. I travelled straight from my work in Fleet Street to Chartwell. It was summer weather. I was wearing old clothes, and was hot and tired from the bustle and stir of the presses.

Churchill was in his garden. He was dressed up in some ancient and subfusc costume which made him look like a genial Michelin tyre advertisement come to life. He was building a wall, and handling the bricks with an enthusiasm which I could easily detect and with a skill which I found it harder to judge—though the wall seemed straight enough.

He had a party of distinguished guests coming to dinner. He insisted on my staying, a black crow among gilded birds of paradise, an inky journalist in grey bags among white ties and tiaras. Yet I was made to feel the most welcome of all the guests. Churchill has a great-heartedness, a warmth and a simplicity in private life which explains the rock-ribbed loyalty of his friends.

He fetched his own shaving tackle for me and stood over me in his private bathroom while I washed, brushed, scraped and made myself presentable. He showed all the comradeship and solicitude of an elder brother, eager for my sake, not his own, that I should appear to best advantage among his friends. It was a revealing sidelight on the character of this citizen of fate.

At that period Churchill was almost at the ebb of his fortunes. He was mellow, genial, philosophical and wise. Lord Beaverbrook, in writing of Churchill, has recorded his opinion that "Churchill down" is the most charming of companions. But "Churchill on the top of the wave has in him the stuff of which tyrants are made."

I remember that Lord Baldwin was on the point of

retiring from the Premiership. Churchill had many reasons for being bitter with Lord Baldwin. He had been in the British Cabinet before Lord Baldwin entered Parliament at all. He had seen the older, slower, steadier man start from far behind, catch him up and outstrip him in the race for power. Yet Churchill was not bitter.

He said to me after dinner that night: "Baldwin is as clever as a Redskin. He will go down to Bewdley, and on Friday nights, or whenever it is that he dances, he will prance around his wigwam pole with my bleeding scalp dangling at his belt."

He laughed without rancour. It was said with lightness and in tones which Lord Baldwin himself would have heard without taking offence.

Later Churchill spoke of the things deep in his heart. He spoke with the smouldering fire of a visionary about the need to destroy the Nazis. He felt war was inevitable —and the sooner it was over, the sooner to sleep.

This big idea had gripped him entirely, just as Hitler and Lenin had been gripped by their ideas. It stirred me to meet the explosive force of a master passion in an age when most Britons regarded enthusiasm with suspicion.

As a result of that evening in his home, one thing became perfectly clear to me. I had doubts as to whether this simple and single idea "The Nazis must be destroyed" was adequate by itself to build a new world. But I had no doubt at all that as an organiser of victory against the Nazis Churchill would be unsurpassed.

I did not want war. I did not yet quit my hopes of peace. But if war had to be our lot and portion, I wanted Churchill. I can see him now, a sombre and brooding figure bidding me farewell from his doorway in the darkness of that summer night. Looked upon by the majority of his countrymen as a spent force, he was heavy with his own sense of impending destiny.

From that time, I worked hard to support Churchill —in public with my pen when I was allowed to do so and in private with my tongue whether I was allowed to do so or not. Even after the outbreak of war, when Chamberlain was Premier and some still hoped for an accommodation with the Nazis, I got into disgrace in certain quarters for asserting that Churchill must become Premier at the earliest possible moment.

A book called *Guilty Men* was published. Over 200,000 copies of it were sold. It flayed some of the public men who had frittered away the time in "the years which the locusts had eaten"—while the Nazi power grew.

Many people said this book played its part in assisting Churchill's rise to the pinnacle of popularity and public esteem. Some alleged that I had something to do with the writing of it.

Anyhow, Guilty or Innocent as I may be, Churchill grew in power.

He rode to destiny. His big idea bears this resemblance to the big ideas of Hitler and Lenin. Everything which stands in its way has to be destroyed. That is part of the price of a war like this.

Churchill is the one man in my lifetime who has been able to mobilise the British people to a passion comparable with the passion of other nations for their ideologies.

"The Nazis must be destroyed." True enough. But after their destruction, what happens to the big idea? It is great. But is it adequate to our age?

Rome had the slogan "Carthage must be destroyed." Carthage was destroyed. Presently Rome fell too. She had not the sustained initiative of a selfless patriotism to hold her country together after the external danger was removed.

CHAPTER IX

SOMETHING HIT ME

CHURCHILL'S best friend was the first and late Lord Birkenhead.

When I was at Oxford Birkenhead showed interest in me, because I was both a footballer and a member of his old college, Wadham. He gave me some advice. I took it—and have regretted it ever since. But that is another story.

Birkenhead was a buccaneer, a gay adventurer. I heard plenty about him from my Oxford scout, or servant, who had looked after him when he was an undergraduate. The scout's name was Smith. That was Birkenhead's name also before he was ennobled.

The scout used to take work as temporary butler during the vacations. Once a telegram arrived for Smith, Wadham College, offering him a two-month job as footman in Scotland. This telegram was opened by the undergraduate, not the scout.

Birkenhead-to-be was short of cash at the time. So he went to Scotland and did the job which had been intended for his servant.

Birkenhead said that life still offered golden, glittering prizes to those with sharp swords. Also, of his political opponents, that he had beaten them with brains, and that if they chose to put up the barricades, he would slit their soft white throats for them.

This spirit describes my own in those inter-war years, except that I should probably have been on the opposite side of the barricades to that of Lord Birkenhead.

My sword was sharp. I fought for the gold and the

glitter of wealth, power and reputation. I slit the soft
white throats of those who stood in my pathway as
frequently and effectively with my pen as I was able.

I was always searching for something. Call it what
you will. It is hard to put a name to it. I named it
Happiness. Looking back, I believe I was in search of
some master passion, some great ideal to which I could
wholly give myself, which would provide a motive and
force for my living and by which the world could be
remade.

I sought it in my work, my home, my ambitions.
And though I received much from all these things, and
gave much to them also, yet the fulness of my heart's
desire remained unsatisfied.

All the time Lenin was bidding for me and millions
with his big idea of a super-class.

Hitler was bidding for me and millions with his big
idea of a super-race.

So were the politicians, planners and pundits of Westminster who paraded their panaceas between the wars.

But somehow, though I liked some of these ideas better
than the others, I remained heart-whole.

What were my deepest convictions? They say that an
Englishman is no more ready than a burglar to discuss
his convictions. At any rate, my convictions in those
inter-war years were not such as would make my friends
uncomfortable. Certainly they were not such as would
make me uncomfortable either.

The great General Booth, after talking with Churchill
and studying him closely in his younger day, remarked
that he was badly in need of what old-fashioned people
described as conversion. Probably Booth would have
said the same of me—and I should have been as irritated
and disdainful of his observation as I suspect Churchill
may have been.

Anyway, it was in this spirit and from such a background that I strode out to meet the adventure of my life. In half an hour I found the secret which for years had eluded me and millions like me.

I was on the look-out for news, as every good journalist must be. I was fresh from a meeting with some of the leading statesmen of Britain, at which many of the things said had incensed me by their complacency. At luncheon I launched into a criticism of these statesmen.

The man sitting next me said, "You know, criticism is not much good by itself. Any fool can do it, and most fools do."

Then he went on, "I believe the men of the future are those who match their criticism with cure."

I looked at this fellow with asperity. I was not accustomed to be spoken to in such a manner by people unknown to myself and therefore of small importance to me. I said sharply, "Death is the only permanent cure for some of our politicians."

He replied, "That is the mistake so many people like you make, if I may say so. Everybody says the world ought to be different. But only a few people know how it can happen."

I laughed with scorn and said, "You're not suggesting you have got some secret that will change the world, are you?"

This man answered, "No. I'm not suggesting anything. I'm telling you. It is the forgotten factor that will turn the tide of history. It will affect the future more fundamentally than the discovery of wireless, print, steam or the internal combustion engine affected the past. It is not theory. It is fact. I have tried it."

I took a good look at this fellow. I saw he was no crank. Indeed he seemed one of the sanest men I ever had met. I realised that if what he told me was true, it was the most important thing in the world, the biggest newspaper story I ever had had the luck to find. I asked him questions.

Later on, after luncheon was over, this man told me his secret, and how it could become available to me. I decided to make trial of the adventure.

Down on the Suffolk farm where Doë and I live, I sometimes have to carry great sacks of corn on my back across the barn floor. The sacks weigh two hundred-weight. As you carry them forward, you get used to the weight of them. But when you set them down, suddenly you realise the intolerable load you have been carrying. Your feet seem to leave the surface of the ground, and you float on air.

It was a similar sensation of easement, relief and release which I felt the morning after that luncheon party. A woman M.P. who disliked me and for years had not spoken to me, stopped dead in her tracks in the Lobby of the House of Commons when she saw me. "Good heavens, Peter Howard," she said, "what have you been doing? You look ten years younger."

And besides feeling different and looking different, I saw differently. The shifting, whirling kaleidoscope of life suddenly slipped into perspective.

I saw in a flash the clue which in the long run would give mankind the answer to each last baffling question.

I saw where I and millions like me had lost our way and also how we could begin forthwith to build the sort of world all men and nations long for.

At last I had come to the end of my old journey and the beginning of the new. I had discovered an idea bigger than all the rest.

Chapter X

WHATISIT?

THE scales fell away from my eyes. I saw both cause and cure of our troubles.

I was reminded of the mystery of Rose.

Rose was the name of my first lady-love.

She used to give me tit-bits from my mother's store cupboard. Once she popped a round pat of butter into my mouth when my nurse was not looking. I can still remember my feelings of terror and delight as I gulped it down.

Also Rose was able to balance herself on a bicycle without falling off and without moving forward. She lent adventure and fragrance to my childhood days.

One morning men came and put straw in the street outside our front door. Rose was ill. My nurse told me that the straw was to prevent her being disturbed by the clatter of hooves and the crunch of iron-rimmed wheels on the roadway.

A few days later, Rose was taken away in a box to be buried. It was my first encounter with death. It was vivid, mysterious and terrifying.

I heard that Rose had been killed by something called influenza. The destruction of Rose by influenza seemed to me even more senseless and savage than the destruction of millions by the Great War which was shaking the earth at the time.

The newspapers were full of names like Hill 60, Passchendaele and the Menin Road. They gave accounts of battles in which thousands lost their lives daily. But they said nothing about influenza which had killed my poor Rose.

The newspapers were wrong. Rose was one of the early victims of that wave of influenza which swept the world at the close of the Great War. Insidious, silent, hidden and world-wide, it carried off more victims than the war itself.

What is wrong with the world to-day? Some say that war is the cause of all the trouble. But the world was wrong before war broke out. The end of war does not mark the end of all our troubles.

The world is sick unto death. It is suffering from a disease. That disease remains unrecognised by the newspapers, although already its victims number tens of millions and it is active in the heart of every nation, including our own.

It infects homes. Two young folk fall in love and marry. Both are decent people. Both truly intend to make a success of their life together. But before long, they are drifting apart. Either they separate, or they stay together, nervous and irritable, bringing up a family in an atmosphere of bully and drudge.

The disease infects business and industry. An employer takes on a new workman. Both men mean to treat the other well. The first day on the job goes splendidly. But before long their relationship sours.

The man says, "There's not much in this for me, blooming slave-driver."

The master says, "He never does a stroke of work when my back is turned."

On a larger scale, millions of workmen long to do a good day's work in exchange for a fair return. Thousands of employers want to treat their people as well as they can. These desires are genuine. And both could be realised. Yet somehow bosses and workers find them-

selves at the place where both sides organise to discredit
a nd fight each other and spend half their time and energy
in doing so.

This disease causes situations where we have seen
the fish shops in East London empty while at Grimsby the
trawler crews throw their catch back into the sea because
they cannot find a market for it.

In Europe we have seen millions go short of food and
miners on the dole, while in South America they use
maize and coffee instead of coal as locomotive fuel.
In Russia peasants starve, while Canadian and American
farmers are hard up owing to a glut of wheat which has
depressed the world market.

Finally, the vast majority of men and women in all
nations hate war and long for peace. Yet somehow
the world goes to war again.

All these are symptoms of this strange disease from
which mankind is suffering. We all mean so well, yet
somehow things go wrong. What is the common
denominator of all these disasters?

The two chief symptoms by which you can recognise
the disease which has infected the earth are ingrowing
eyeballs and itching palms.

Ingrowing eyeballs make a man always see Number
One first before he sees his neighbours. Itching palms
are always on the grab.

The disease is commonly called "Gimme" or "Get".
It kills millions dead, though they do not lie down. It
is the subtle philosophy, now world-wide, that makes men
look for happiness in the wrong place. It is a search,
restless, endless for more and more and more of what
does not satisfy.

Like most diseases, Gimme has a long Latin name.
The name is Materialism. According to the Oxford
Dictionary it is "a way of life devoted to material

interests." So Gimme is a way of life. It is not what we say but how we live. It is a wrong attitude to things.

In my own case, my attitude to money, personal advancement and sex were wrong. There was nothing wrong with these things in themselves. But when my attitude to them became one of grab and Gimme I became part of the disease of the age.

When my attitude to things goes wrong, my desire for them controls and possesses me. Then that desire affects my actions. For fear enters in—fear that I shall not get what I want or that somebody else will take from me what I have.

This fear is sometimes called greed.

The trouble with Materialism is that it never has worked, and never will. It always looks attractive as a blueprint. When you put it on the road it always crashes.

It is based on the phoney belief that men can run the world God made. God made the world. But He did not design it to run on the spirit of Gimme. That is the spirit man has been trying to put into the engine ever since. So we get breakdowns.

The signs of Gimme are division, broken homes, lockouts, strikes, unemployment, race riots, wars.

Also dictatorships. For Materialism breeds two broad types of men. It breeds the softness which will accept dictation, and the ambition which dictates. It breeds the apathetic individual, irresponsible, discontented and inactive, who says all the time, "Why doesn't somebody do something?" It breeds the bitter, forceful and ambitious spirit which is out to smash the powers that stand in the way and to take control.

In democratic countries, whose greatness was founded upon the conception of the equality of all men because their spirits have equal value in the eyes of God Who created them, Materialism pursues an additional strategy.

It appeals to man's love of comfort and ease.

It tells him that everybody is selfish—that you have to be selfish to get along.

It says that anything a man enjoys is the right thing for him to have.

So men and nations become less equipped, morally and physically, to resist the challenge of aggressive Materialism, whether of Left or Right.

They prefer peace at any price to the strenuous spiritual warfare which is the price of lasting peace.

Soon they come to prefer peace to moral principles. "Throw a dog a bone of somebody else's territory to keep it quiet," they say.

So Materialism, which makes the dictator nations formidable, makes the democratic nations feeble. For the "Isms" are the children of Materialism, but democracy is the child of a Christian faith.

Materialism is meat for one but poison for the other.

Materialism inevitably causes dictatorship and war. When all men are on the get, chaos results and the strong man steps in.

Men on the get bump into each other.

So do nations on the get.

The world once more crashes to disaster.

CHAPTER XI

THE WAR OF IDEAS

THERE is nothing new in Materialism. It is as old as the story of the apple in the Garden of Eden.

But the new factor about Materialism in our modern world is this. For the first time in history Materialism is consciously and cleverly organised, nationally and internationally, by men who are committed to gain power on the widest possible scale.

Materialism to-day is a world-wide, militant and organised force. Yet many of us, full of idealism and vague goodwill as we may be, stay blind to it.

All my life I had loathed narrow-mindedness. By the phrase "narrow-minded", I meant those who disapproved of what I did. As a Fleet Street man, I fancied myself broad-minded, by which I meant that I would not interfere with others, if they let me live as I liked.

But suddenly I saw exactly how broad my own mind was. Indeed I could draw a diagram of my mind on paper. It was as broad as the letter "I", neither more nor less. For years I had thought of everything and everybody in terms of how they affected myself.

This was natural enough for a man whose master passion, like the master passion of millions, was to get on in the world. Up and down that single monotonous track, "I", my mind had wandered, ceaselessly to and fro, until a groove had been worn into which my thinking had sunk and I was incapable of looking in any direction but the one of self-interest which I had chosen.

I was blinded by my own materialism. I never saw

the organised militant Materialism which, on the march, causes war and revolution. Why? I was part of it.

Materialism, the spirit of Gimme in the hearts of men, is the mother of wars. It is also the mother of the "Isms". Karl Marx, for example, was a man of ambition. He believed that the Gimme in man, his desire to grab as much as possible for himself from this world while he was in it, was man's chief motive of life. Marx thought that to be the natural and right motive. He urged the masses to band together and seize by force the things they wanted.

So he built up a leadership of ambitious and embittered men and a world-wide following of those who were too soft to say *No* to material desire. He integrated the spirit of Gimme in the heart of man into a political creed and world-wide revolutionary movement. "Marxism is Materialism Militant," said Lenin.

So is Hitlerism. So is Fascism, and every "Ism".

I, and millions like me in Britain, disapproved of the "Isms" in the inter-war years. Yet we were ourselves a part of that Materialism, that spirit of Gimme, which made the march of the "Isms" possible and inevitable.

The militant Materialists deluded millions in Britain just as they enlisted millions on the Continent. There are more ways of organising Materialism than by the continental techniques of swastika and sickle.

In Britain Materialism was organised by those who hoped to gain power, cash or pleasure by it.

Apart from the recognised apostles of the "Isms" in these islands it was organised, for instance, by certain sections of Fleet Street who built circulation on smut and sensation, presenting news and comment in a way which would suit advertising revenue.

Equally it was organised by certain business circles and some leaders of Labour who exploited the market or

their associations for personal power—and by an influ-
ential group of intellectuals who degraded art into self-
expression and conduct to the level of the farmyard, in
order to make money for themselves and fortify themselves in their own illicit pleasures.

This materialist front in Britain was as real as the
materialist front against which we declared war.

To-day, as I write, we are at war. And we shall be
at war long after Germany and Japan are beaten.

For we are fighting two wars. Both are fought on a
world front. One is the WAR OF ARMS. It involves
tanks, guns, planes, armies and alliances.

The other is the WAR OF IDEAS. It involves faiths,
standards of conduct and philosophies of life.

The war of ideas began before the war of arms and it
will continue long after the war of arms is ended.

It is possible to be on the same side in the war of arms
but with different objectives in the war of ideas. Russia,
for example, is at the time of writing an ally in the war
of arms. Her military power has turned the tide of
battle. But is Russia's idea our idea?[1] We may fight
and win the war of arms together while still reserving
the right, as friends, to differ upon what is the best big
idea in matters of faith and government.

.   .   .   .   .

We fight a total war. The aim of total warfare must
be total victory. For that we need to win the war of
ideas as well as the war of arms. A mere disapproval
of the "Isms" will never conquer them. For the "Isms"

---

[1] There have been many pronouncements on the subject of
Soviet policy. If we turn to authoritative utterances by official
spokesmen and founders, Stalin, speaking of the new Russian
Constitution of 1936, says, "The State is a machine in the hands
of the governing class, for suppressing the resistance of its class
antagonists. In this respect, the dictatorship of the proletariat
differs in no way essentially from that of any other class."

are new and powerful faiths, the organised and militant established churches of Materialism, for which millions risk everything. A powerful faith, even if it is a faith in a false god, will always brush aside and smash down men and nations which have no fighting faith at all. Any religion is stronger than no religion.

When totalitarian Materialism, or the organised spirit of Gimme, becomes a militant way of life, then it bids to occupy the spiritual territory of other nations, to alter their way of life, as definitely as do the armed forces of aggression.

So victory in the war of arms, though essential, is not adequate by itself to produce total victory. For you cannot win the war of ideas by armed force.

You cannot shoot an idea dead. Men have often tried to do so and often failed. A victory of *our* arms will not necessarily conquer *their* faith any more than a victory of *their* arms conquered the faith of the free in many an occupied territory.

It is conceivable that we might win the war of arms and lose the war of ideas. In that case we should find established on a world front after victory the way of life we went to war to beat.

As I began to think in these terms, I saw clearly the nature of the struggle in which we are engaged. I saw that the big question of contemporary history is, "What idea will dominate the world when the war is over?"

A victory of U.S.A., Russia, China and Britain over Germany and Japan cannot answer that question. For these victor nations do not all share the same ideas.

Nor do all the citizens in any one victor nation share the same ideas. For while the war of arms is *between* nations, the war of ideas runs *through* nations. In the war of ideas we fight against a spirit of Materialism, a spirit of Gimme, a spirit which breeds wars and "Isms", a wrong spirit in the heart of man. The battle line in the war of ideas runs through every factory, farm, home and life in every land.

Whenever I am on the get, out for myself at the expense of the other fellow, the other class, the other race, I become a fifth columnist in the war of ideas. For I am part of the very Materialism which creates and makes formidable the "Isms".

Men become infected with the conviction that to get as much as possible matters more than anything else in the world. They come to represent a "Get" front, a fifth column centre, and wield an intangible, invisible force which powerfully impacts the spirit of their nation and their neighbours.

It was this "Get" front, the spirit of Materialism in me and millions like me, which made possible the world situation between the wars. In Britain we never dealt with it, because we never fully recognised the war of ideas.

We saw plenty of things in the "Isms" which we did not like. We hated the symptoms of the disease. But we never saw that the elements of the disease itself were in our own national blood-stream.

As a democracy, we are particularly equipped to turn the tide in the war of ideas. All our greatness and the enduring principles of our democratic heritage have sprung from the Christian faith of generations of our ancestors. That has been Christianity's gift to the world—the conceptions of honesty, moral principle, God-control, fairplay, freedom—lived for and died for by reformers, martyrs, soldiers, statesmen for two thousand years.

Democracy's destiny must be to turn back the oncoming forces of militant Materialism in the war of ideas as effectively as alone Britain turned the tide of armed aggression in the Battle of the Skies after Dunkirk.

Chapter XII

MAN OF THE FUTURE

THERE are two kinds of human greatness. There are the men of the moment—and the men of the future.

The men of the moment are symbols of their age. They are flung up to power by the trends, emotions and opportunities of the times they live in.

The men of the future have that prophetic quality which creates the next age. They fashion the times in which their children and children's children will live.

Cæsar was a man of the moment. Paul was a man of the future.

In the same way Napoleon bestrode the world as the man of the moment in his day, giving a marching might and impetus to the revolutionary doctrines of his age. But John Wesley, riding his horse from end to end of Britain, at work from four o'clock in the morning until late at night, was the man of the future. His achievement, not fully recognised until long after his death, was to bring a spirit into Britain strong enough to stand the shock of revolutionary armies and ideas, and to transform the social fabric of the nation.

In the year 1921, while Lenin reigned in glory at the Kremlin and before Hitler's hour had struck, a man climbed into a train at Hartford, Connecticut, to go to Washington. He had been invited by one of the British delegates to attend the Disarmament Conference.

He was destined to become the spearpoint in our day and age of the one idea big enough to outmatch and outmarch the "Isms" of Materialism. His name was Frank Buchman—the man of the future. He was at that time in a well-paid, secure job. He spent six months of the year teaching at an American college, and six months travelling the world as he chose.

It was a happy, interesting and safe life.

Yet as he climbed into the sleeper that night, Frank Buchman felt uneasy. He is a man of prophetic prescience. He saw the fatuity of all the satisfaction around him. Peace was won, Prosperity was ahead, said everybody, and the Disarmament Conference in session which would establish goodwill on the earth.

But Buchman knew that the world had not been changed by the World War. The world was the same as it had been at the beginning of the war. In the cheers and enthusiasm which encircled that Disarmament Conference at Washington, equalling the uproar and ardour which had heralded the declaration of war, Buchman saw the same futility. "A war to end war," "A land fit for heroes to live in," "A world made safe for democracy,"—he recognised them as phrases, and nothing else. They were the words without the music, clamour without content.

Half the world was still on top and the other half submerged on the bottom. This was true of nations and their nationals. Fear, greed, ambition, hatred—all were still present in full measure. Not one basic cause of war had been destroyed by war. Materialism was on the march on a world front, about to breed the "Isms". The war of arms had been won and lost. The war of ideas had yet to be waged.

It was borne upon Frank Buchman's mind, attuned to the practice of getting guidance from God, that there was no short cut to a new age. He was carried through the night sleepless in his berth in the train. A friend of mine once said Buchman tossed and turned on that journey. Buchman, on hearing it, told my friend this was not so.

He declares he lay still throughout that night. Again and again, luminous and clear, the thought shone into his mind, "Resign, Resign, Resign."

As the hours and miles flew by he counted the cost of the decision. And he accepted it.

That decision was to resign his salaried and safe job and to devote the rest of his days to forging an instrument which might remake the world.

Frank Buchman saw in those far-off days of 1921 that some of the cleverest brains in the world were at work to ride to power on the back of Materialism. He saw that for the first time in history a planned strategy for Materialism on a national and global scale was being prepared. He saw that revolutionaries of both Left and Right in many countries were resolved to harness the massive force of the selfishness of man, all the Gimme of the human heart, to power programmes.

Buchman realised that nothing except the fire of a great awakening on a world front could save humanity from conquest by the oncoming forces of Materialism. He knew that the old-style religious revival was inadequate to stand the shock of the new-style materialistic revolution. A spirit of goodwill without an adequate plan was as useless as a plan without a new spirit to set it on the march.

Frank Buchman saw with prophetic vision that if the Christian forces were to overcome the advancing armies of Materialism they would need a plan to meet a plan, a strategy to meet a strategy, training to meet training, and the superforce and passion of a new spirit to conquer the force and passion of new, revolutionary ideas.

Here is the measure of his achievement. He has done for the best side of human nature what the materialist revolutionaries of Left and Right have done for the worst side of human nature. These men, the men of the hour, have taken the ideas of lust, greed and grab, which always had existed in the world, and given them for the first time an international strategy and framework. They gave the ideas legs and the legs began to march.

Buchman, the man of the future, has taken the ideas of honesty, purity, unselfishness and love, of the guidance of God and the possibility of a change in human nature, which had existed in the world since men killed the carpenter's son, and given them in our time an international strategy and framework—Moral Re-Armament. He gave these ideas legs, and they are on the march to-day.

It is a tremendous revolutionary achievement, that this one man, since he took that decision on the night train to Washington, has built up and integrated a world front, extending into over sixty countries, against the force of Materialism.

How was it done? Frank Buchman is a man of simple faith. He believes that God has a plan for the world. He says, "When man listens, God speaks. When man obeys, God acts. When men change, nations change."

From the day he began to build up a world instrument to turn the tide of history his principle has been "World-remaking and nation-changing through life-changing."

First he went to Oxford and there found and trained the men needed for the leadership of the work in many lands. Then, with his teams, he travelled the world. Wherever he went he left behind him trained, disciplined groups of selfless fighters, a united supernational force, unshakable in their loyalty and bound together by the greater vision of a world remade.

It was in South Africa that Frank Buchman's teams were first given the name Oxford Group which has stuck to them ever since. A black railway porter, knowing that a party of people had reserved a compartment to travel from Grahamstown, asked who they were. He was told, "A group of people from Oxford." So he scrawled the words "Oxford Group" in chalk on the railway carriage door. When the newspaper reporters saw it, they took up the story. That was the beginning of the name.

Frank Buchman and the Oxford Group fought against the easy blindness of Materialism in its many forms— the unrealistic devotion to peace, the apathetic antipathy to wrong, the heartless acceptance of unemployment, the selfish enjoyment of prosperity—these he fought with all his power.

Men of insight began to turn to him. Discerning enemies began to oppose him. The world battle that always develops when a man of moral convictions arises was joined. The Oxford Group, spread by then into sixty countries around the world, became the focus of this battle.

Frank Buchman's own definition still stands from early days when first the conception of a change of world policy through change in the spirit of men gripped him. "The Oxford Group is a Christian revolution," he said, "whose concern is vital Christianity. Its aim is a new social order under the dictatorship of the Spirit of God, making for better human relationships, for unselfish co-operation, for cleaner business, cleaner politics, for the elimination of political, industrial and racial antagonisms. . . . Upon a foundation of changed lives, permanent reconstruction is assured. Apart from changed lives, no civilisation can endure."

The Oxford Group was running a race against time. The new illumination of its message became daily more vital as the black clouds of war began once again to gather over Europe and the world. In that time of crisis Moral Re-Armament was conceived. "The Oxford Group is the leadership. Moral Re-Armament is the philosophy." So one man has described it.

In June, 1938, at the East Ham Town Hall, packed by hundreds of dockers, shopkeepers, railwaymen, the ordinary people who, under God, could become remakers of the world, the campaign for Moral Re-Armament was initiated and launched. Frank Buchman said at that great meeting, "We, the Remakers of the World— is that not the thinking and willing of the ordinary man? . . . Every man, woman and child must be enlisted, every home become a fort. Our aim should be that everyone has not only enough of the necessities of life, but that he has a legitimate part in bringing about this moral re-armament. . . . We can, we must, and we will generate a moral and spiritual force that is powerful enough to remake the world."

Across the world the phrase "Moral Re-Armament" spread, and the philosophy followed. It gathered the momentum of a mighty world movement,[1] building

[1] *The Congressional Record*, official record of the proceedings of the United States Congress, of June 8th, 1939, contains a speech by Senator Truman, describing the launching of Moral Re-Armament in America at the Constitution Hall, Washington. Senator Truman mentions messages received for the meeting from President Roosevelt, General Pershing, former President Hoover, Secretary of State Cordell Hull, while a third of the United States Senate and a large body of Congressmen acted as sponsors. Similar support came on this occasion from 240 British Members of Parliament and representative groups in eight other European Parliaments and from the Dominions, and from Labour and industrial leaders throughout the world. Said Senator Truman, "It is rare in these days to find something which will unite men and nations on a plane above conflict of party, class or political philosophy."

Prime Minister Curtin of Australia recently adjourned Parliament for a performance of the M R A revue, *Battle For Australia*, put on at his request in the Parliament House, Canberra, and Deputy Premier Nash of New Zealand said during his visit to America for the I.L.O. Conference of 1944, of which he was Chairman, "If we are determined to walk along the road the men and women of M R A show us, the sacrifices made by our soldiers will be worth while, and we will be on the road to building something better than we have ever built before." In the Far East, M R A has had the support of Generalissimo and Madame Chiang Kai-shek.

Into millions of hearts and lives the spirit which alone could make the peace which followed the war lasting.

As the philosophy of Moral Re-Armament advanced on a world front opposition to it from certain quarters increased. At the height of the war against Hitler, Tojo and Mussolini, a high-ranking American Army officer analysed the type of opposition encountered by it. He noted that it drew the fire equally of Nazis and Communists; of the extreme Right and the extreme Left in politics; of aggressive atheists and narrow ecclesiastics. It had been charged by radicals with being militarist and by war-mongers with being pacifist. Certain elements in Labour denounced it as anti-union; certain elements in Management as pro-union.

In Britain MRA was accused by some of being a brilliantly clever front for Fascism; in Germany and Japan of being a super-intelligent arm of the British and American Secret Service. One day a section of the Press would announce that MRA was defunct and the next that it numbered nearly the entire membership of the British Cabinet at the time of Munich, and was responsible for engineering Hitler's attack upon Russia!

"Nothing," this officer concluded, "but a potentially vast moral and spiritual reformation of global proportions could possibly be honoured by antagonisms so venomous and contradictory in character, and so world-wide in scope."

This is an accurate diagnosis. For to-day the spirit of Moral Re-Armament has created in many different lands an unshakable framework which has withstood the shocks of peace and war. It has survived the strains of separation and loss. It was the steel which held nations together under the domination of alien armies and creeds. It stands to-day on a world front, the force of the future.

Frank Buchman, the man of the future, gave up more
for his big idea than the revolutionary leaders of Left
and Right, the men of the hour, gave up for theirs. He
risked all he had in this world. And he offered one
thing which the Materialists did not. He sacrificed all
hope of power and glory in his lifetime.

On the ordinary level of human achievement, Frank
Buchman could have won recognition in this world.
Even his bitterest opponents admit that he is a man of
outstanding ability. Yet Buchman's life has been poured
out in his sustained and selfless efforts to raise up around
him and in many countries shoulder to shoulder leadership. For he knows that an instrument capable, under
God, of remaking the world, must be strong enough to
survive more than one man's lifetime.

In another way, Frank Buchman's approach to world
problems differs fundamentally from that of the man of
the hour. Other leaders of this age of ours take human
nature as it is, and make the best or worst of it. They
exploit its weakness, they debase it or in some cases
stimulate it by passion and oratory for some brief purpose
or supreme task.

But Frank Buchman, man of the future, never for one
minute accepts human nature as it is. He sets human
nature to its basic destiny of change and sustained
advance.

Others put things before people in their programme.
He puts people before things. He says, "If you have
people, you have a plan." He does not look on the masses
as people to despise, to use and to cajole. Like his fellow-
countryman, Abraham Lincoln, he has a great love for
the ordinary man, and a faith in his destiny. The man
in the street, changed by the superforce of the spirit, will,
he says, be the man of the future.

His statesmanship grows, not from theories, but out of

a love and understanding of men. He knows people, and much of his life has been given to meeting deep human needs. Consequently there is perhaps no man to-day who is so much loved by so many. Once when he had heart trouble, the leader of 50,000 aircraft workers wired to him, "What can you expect when you take the whole of America into your heart?" Another labour leader saw the wire and said, "America? He has taken the whole human race into his heart."

He is a man in all things uniquely original. He has brought a new thinking into politics, but founded no party. He has brought new life into the churches, but founded no church. He has built a world-wide front based not on dues and guarantees but on his boundless faith in God's provision. In a materialistic age he works and expects others to work without financial reward. He has bound together countless thousands in all lands, not by any membership, but by the precious bond of a common heart and mind. He has a plan to perpetuate his work, without founding any organisation.

Whence do all these things spring? Very simply they come from the Cross of Christ. That is the master key to understand his work, for it is the master pattern of his life. As James Watt's work would be meaningless without steam power or Edison's without electric power, his would mean nothing without the Cross of Christ. "For too many," he has said, "it has become a symbol and not an experience." It is the hope of nations. It is the one power that can change human nature. At the same time it is the beacon light to the nations in the war of ideas, the battle of the ideologies for the soul of mankind. It is the great perspective given in history. It provides at once a force and a philosophy. It is God's answer to man's Materialism.

Chapter XIII

SUCH MEN ARE DANGEROUS

HERE is the situation in the world. First, there are the legionaries of the new spirit. They are veterans of the shape of things to come, pioneering the super-force which changes human nature. They see the war of ideas clearly. They fight unitedly on a world front to usher in a new age of new men and new women, to answer the oncoming might of Materialism with the fire of a great awakening.

Then there are the regiments of militant Materialism, the shock-troops of the "Isms". They, too, see the war of ideas clearly. They also fight on a world front to establish the oldest form of jungle rule, the godless dictatorship of the world by one section of it.

Finally, there are the Missing and Misty Millions. For a long time, I was one of them. They are the lost souls of history. They have yet to recognise the war of ideas. They say that the world is in a mess, but do not believe they had anything to do with putting it there, and cannot see that they have any part to play in pulling it out again. They all want to have the other fellow changed, and are all waiting for the other fellow to begin.

Because they do not see the war of ideas clearly, they are often unconsciously made the dupes and tools of militant Materialism. The Materialists constantly strive to win these Missing and Misty Millions to their side.

The Materialists' strategy is to dupe the ordinary man. For if they are to ride to power or opulence they must ride on his back, having convinced him that they are offering him a lift to the top of the hill. So they have mastered the technique of the confidence trickster, the card-sharper or the obliging gentleman in a flash tweed suit who sells you a gold brick for half a crown. They persuade the ordinary man that it is his interest which they have at heart. In fact, they use him for their own gain.

The Materialists work with anybody so long as unconsciously he serves their ends. Thus Hitler used men as stepping stones in his rise to power, and then killed them when they finally saw where he was leading them. Then in various lands the Marxists work with clergy, monarchists, intellectuals and liberals—anybody at all who will further their ends—and liquidate them when they feel strong enough to do so. And it is all done under the camouflage of fine words about progress, liberation, self-expression and such like. The first Materialist of all, the snake in the Garden of Eden, did his work in the cause of Higher Education.

The ordinary man who is allured by the bright promises of the Materialists is like the fish which swallows the bait. He loses his liberty. He goes into the pot of the militant and organised materialist forces, to increase their feast of power or pounds or pleasure.

Throughout history he is a pawn in their game.

Some militant Materialists are frank enough to say so. Hitler bluntly declares his contempt for the mentality of the masses (though it raised him to power), and says you must manage the ordinary fellow by ruthless propaganda—he will always swallow the big lie, even if he hesitates over the little lie.

Lenin is even more explicit. In *What Is To Be Done?* he urges that every grievance in the heart of the ordinary man must be stimulated and exploited for party ends. "Our task," he says, "is to utilise every manifestation of discontent, and to collect and utilise every grain of even rudimentary protest. Is there a single class of the population in which no individuals, groups or circles are to be found who are discontented and therefore inaccessible to our propaganda?"

You get similar exploitation of the masses by organised materialist influences in Britain, though they are not always so frank about it.

Thus some newspapers peddle pornography at a penny a time for the sake of sales and dividends.

Some big financial interests regard people as things, and use the masses as a mere source of revenue.

There are intellectual, artistic and political circles which for years have propagated their ideas of licence among the ordinary men and women of Britain, so that they may have company and justification for their own pleasures in sex.[1] Opinion which drove men out of public life for gross immorality was dangerous to them.

There are the agitators who promote industrial unrest to increase their political power rather than to improve the lot of the working classes.

All these and many more Materialists in Britain exploit the ordinary man. They use us and they bring out the worst in us.

[1] Aldous Huxley in his book *Ends and Means* describes this process of mind in himself and his contemporaries: "I had motives for not wanting the world to have a meaning, consequently assumed that it had none and was able without any difficulty to find satisfying reasons for this assumption. . . . The philosopher who finds no meaning in the world is not concerned exclusively with a problem in pure metaphysics; he is also concerned to prove there is no valid reason why he personally should not do as he wants, or why his friends should not seize political power and govern in the way they find most advantageous to themselves. . . . For myself, as no doubt, for most of my contemporaries, the philosophy of meaninglessness was essentially an instrument of liberation. The liberation we desired was simultaneously liberation from a certain political and economic system and liberation from a certain system of morality. We objected to the morality because it interfered with our sexual freedom."

In *What I Believe* Tolstoi portrays a similar situation that existed in Russian intellectual circles at the end of the last century.

They have three main tactics in dealing with us.

Tactic Number 1. They play on weakness. A demand is growing for sexual instruction as part of school and university teaching. A fine scheme—until it gets into the wrong hands, as sometimes it does. Then the secret idea back of it is not that our young men and women shall learn self-discipline but that they shall be taught to indulge themselves with a decreased risk of venereal disease or babies.

Then there is a steady campaign to make divorce easier and swifter, and some of its advocates are no doubt sincere people. But these sincere people fail to recognise the final objectives of the militant Materialists. That is to degrade the whole conception of marriage from a Christian institution into a civil contract.

It is the same policy that made Hitler's Nazis take with them immense stocks of pornographic literature when they marched into Poland. This was a main weapon of their assault on the morale of occupied Poland.

In the same way, before the war, Marxist agitators were active in the European schools and universities and elsewhere, giving lectures and free "education" on sex. If you can get people soft and unable to say *No* to themselves, they find it difficult to say *No* to you, and their resistance to your big idea is broken down.

Tactic Number 2. The Materialists bid for the Misty Millions by playing on man's capacity to hate. People enjoy hating almost as much as they enjoy lusting. Men like a grievance. They like to have somebody else to blame. It puts them in the right. It makes them feel good.

So the subversive elements get to work. They take a situation like the relationship between Britain and America, and seek to undermine it. "The Yanks are out for what they can get. They care nothing for you," the subversive forces say to Britain. "The British are out for what they can get. They care nothing for you," the subversive forces say to America.

Everything American is sneered at and derided by the subversive forces in Britain. Everything British is sneered at and derided by the subversive forces in America. For these forces know that if these two countries fall out, there is little hope for the rest of the world. So a main aim for them in the war of ideas, now being fought on a global scale, is the disruption of Anglo-American unity.

Also the subversive elements strive to create hatred between race and race, class and class. The battle line of division runs through every home, wife against husband, parents against children. It runs through industry, worker against boss, Capital against Labour.

It splits nations into sections. It sets the sections battling to control each other, and the nations battling to control each other too.

Bewilderment, chaos, division, disunity—it is the objective of militant Materialism to create it everywhere. Disunity gives the "Isms" their opportunity. Every little friction weakens a nation's defences against the invasion of a militant idea. Divide and destroy—that is the age-old strategy of Materialism for men and nations.

Tactic Number 3. The Materialists delude the ordinary fellow by shouting a series of false alternatives and pretending there is no third way. Here are some of them:

Look after Number One first or your number is up.

Grab or go under.

Control the other fellow or be controlled by him.

Support Nazism or you are a Jewish Bolshevist; support Communism or you are a Fascist reactionary.

The unhappy husband or wife must choose between divorce or deadlock; parents between birth control or no control, between spoiling or spanking their children.

Government must choose between controlling Labour by force or coddling it; between bullying or bribing; between favouring Management or liquidating it; between taking all property away from individuals or watching them use it as selfishly as they please.

Management must choose between being brutal or sentimental; Labour between strike action or inaction.

Britain must choose between exploitation or evacuation of her Empire.

The peacemakers between exterminating the aggressors or letting them off.

And the peoples of the world between being oppressed or rising up in bloody revolution.

Of course, there is an answer to these so-called alternatives—the third way of a new spirit that introduces into every equation of hopelessness the new element of change.

The positive forces who pioneer the new spirit offer the greatest danger to the Materialists. For, of course, these pioneers are not fooled by the tactics of playing on weakness and hate or offering false alternatives. So the negative forces of Materialism use different methods against them. They attack them directly, having failed to fool them. They do everything in their power to discredit, misrepresent and destroy them.

That is why Frank Buchman and his men have been ever at the thickest of the fighting in this war of ideas, this battle between M R A and Materialism for the soul of the world. In almost every case, the morally defeated and the extremists of the Left or Right have been back of the assault on M R A.

There is nothing new in it. It is the traditional, age-old strategy of Materialism.

They crucified Christ.

Forty men swore an oath they would never eat nor drink until they killed Paul. St. Francis of Assisi was

D

gaoled by his father. Ignatius Loyola was hounded
from country to country, put on trial and imprisoned.

John Knox was locked up aboard the galleys and
accused of disloyalty to the State. He was sentenced
to death and burned in effigy while he was in hiding.

Throughout history there have always been assaults
against the moral and spiritual forces of the age. To-day
Moral Re-Armament faces a like attack. At the time
they take place, the attackers seem to have the power
and to dominate the scene. But history records the
achievement of those who were attacked.

Few now remember the names of those who locked the
tinker's son in Bedford Gaol for twelve long years—but
all know John Bunyan and his *Pilgrim's Progress*—John
Bunyan, one of our immortal national heroes, who was
locked in a dungeon by us, his fellow citizens, for a fifth
of his lifetime because of his warrior heart.

One feature of the attack of the Materialists on those
who pioneer the new spirit is that they denounce in these
pioneers the quality which is abundant in themselves.

This is called "projection". "I take care to keep
away from that crowd of folk. There's something not
quite nice about them," as the Skunk said to his wife
over the telephone.

If you listen to some of the things people say as they
attack M R A you discover plenty about the critics.

We give ourselves away by our criticisms and pre-
judices. We defend the flaws in ourselves by criticising
them most violently in others.

The war against John Wesley illustrates this clearly.
John Wesley was a Church of England minister who,
when he was almost thirty-five, discovered that his
experience of Christ was inadequate.

His heart was strangely warmed, his own nature was
transformed and he set out to change his nation.

So the attacks began. His own Church led the hue and cry. At one point almost every pulpit in Britain was closed to him.

Mobs broke up his meetings. He was stoned, punched, knocked off his horse, drenched with slops.

He was accused of making money out of his religion, of sensationalising God and of adopting vulgar "methods".

But the most interesting part of the battle against John Wesley concerns his patriotism.

During Wesley's lifetime Britain was hemmed in by enemies. France was on the verge of revolution and dictatorship, seething with new ideas which dismissed God, morals and religion as antiquated superstitions.

In times of national emergency, the easiest way to smear a man's or a movement's reputation is by denouncing them as disloyal. That is the technique always used by persecutors of religion on these occasions.

So Wesley's enemies put around the story, which was widely believed by well-meaning but foolish people, that Wesley was in league with the French, conspiring to land an army of 50,000 on our shores.

Efforts were made to cripple Wesley's work by taking the few colleagues that he had away from him. His enemies succeeded in kidnapping some of them and pressing them into military service while they themselves stopped at home to continue their assault on Wesley.

Of course, the forces most opposed to Wesley in Britain were the forces who sympathised most in their hearts with the new and softer and pagan code of morality which was springing up in France and elsewhere on the Continent. They sensed that Wesley was the spearpoint of attack against the Materialism of his day.

When the war against France came, it was, in fact, an ideological war. "We are at war," said Pitt, "against armed opinions." It would have been quite possible for Britain to win that material war against France and to lose the ideological war by importing France's new totalitarian and godless philosophy of life into Britain.

Instead historians have recorded their conviction, and it is now commonly accepted, that Wesley did much to save his nation from revolution. Lecky, the great historian, says, "His work is of greater historic importance than all the splendid victories by land and sea under Pitt." A modern view given by the American commentator, Mr. Leland DeWitt Baldwin of Pittsburgh University, is, "Wesley rescued the Anglo-Saxon ideal from dry rot, breathed new life into the soul and recreated the conscience of England, armed the land against internal revolt, revived the old zeal for social service, shook together the dry bones of Empire and clothed them with the flesh of understanding, integrity and honest goodwill."

Thus Wesley, dubbed by his enemies as disloyal, was in fact a source of national strength, while self-styled "patriots" who opposed that resurgence of the spirit which was his life work were the source of national weakness.

Incidentally, while Wesley saved Britain from revolution, at the same time he created the seedbed for the biggest advance the working classes of Britain have ever known. From him men like Shaftesbury and Wilberforce drew the inspiration for their vast programme of social reform. And it was from that seedbed of spiritual values which Wesley left behind him that the early pioneers of the Labour movement sprang and grew, through persecution to maturity.

Wesley left one idea behind him, the French Materialists another. Lenin remarked that the men who had inspired himself and Karl Marx were these French Materialists of a previous century.

Chapter XIV

WHO GOES HOME?

MEMORIES of childhood, memories of home—they are the fabric of life. From the far places on land and sea and in the air, men facing loneliness, danger and death have turned their thoughts home again to the echo of unforgotten laughter, the shadow and smile of loved ones around a flickering fire.

Home—the very word is like a deep note of music. For generations Britain's homes were Britain's glory. There all that was richest in character stood revealed.

There secret hopes and yearnings were known and never derided.

There fears, temptations, difficulties were shared and understood.

There was found a loyalty and love which did not depend on success or income or what the rest of the world thought of you.

All the best of a man blossomed in the warmth of his home—whether a cottage or a castle, home was a place of permanence and tenderness, of peace and laughter, a sanctuary, an inspiration, a corner of the earth which a Briton moulded to his best standards and ideals.

Homes inspire men to greatness. What passion burned in the hearts of those who sailed out from these islands across the grey, cold seas and made an Empire? It was the passion to build new homes. And so they pioneered a family of nations.

Homes were at the root of their conception. Homes turned many a wilderness into a community.

Homes have been the backbone of democracy. They

are the assembly line of national character. And character is the strength of the nation. It can be the final bulwark against the impact of Materialism and the "Isms". That is why forces out to destroy democracy attack home life.

As Her Majesty the Queen said in her broadcast to the women of Britain, "Our precious Christian heritage is threatened by adverse influences."

These influences are helped in their attack on home life by the philosophy of defeat in the home which is becoming more and more an accepted part of the British way, so much so that we almost expect instructions upon how to apply for divorce to be printed on the back of the marriage certificate.

People's thinking about homes has been reduced to rubble as effectively as the homes which have been hit by bombs.

"Till death us do part"—that was the motto and challenge of British homes, where loyalty continued to the grave and beyond it, and where children were the links of a perfect married life and love.

Lately the divorce rate has risen, the birth rate sunk, and many homes have become mere filling stations by day and parking places at night.

The couples who cannot get on without each other are being outnumbered by the couples who cannot get on with each other.

Too many homes have a sweet-shop atmosphere. Surfeit has staled the appetite.

Once a song became popular which contained the inspiring and tender declaration:

"When your hair has turned to silver, I will love you just the same."

That sentiment is more of an aspiration than an accomplishment in many homes. It is one measure of the failure of this age and generation. Think of the massed Himalayan range of human frustration and misery and hopelessness piled up in homes where only a dry, withered and enforced relationship remains.

Bare the secret corner of the heart of each married man and woman. How many have said to themselves, "If I had my choice again, I'd never have done it." So many people stride demandingly over the primrose threshold of the orchard of matrimony, grabbing the fruit with greedy hands and moist, trembling lips, while their minds and appetites expect the feast to last a lifetime. Ten years later they have only a sour and shrunken husk to mumble and sometimes secretly despise.

Since Doë and I began our great adventure, many people have asked us what difference it has made to our home. A friend who has known both of us for many years said to me not long ago, "Well, you were happy enough. In fact you were about the happiest of our crowd. Are you happier now?"

Doë is looking over my shoulder as I write these words. It is a sunny morning and her hands and our home are full of cowslips and forget-me-nots. She will stop me if I write a word or sentence which she does not uphold.

Our marriage has been transformed. Our lives have been transformed. We have found together, after all these years of married life, a swifter and more satisfying adventure than any we expected or experienced as we strode forth across that gangway on to Dover Quay, a honeymoon couple with the flush and flame upon us, two days after our wedding.

To-day we know the answer to all those things, great and small, which can and do stain or shadow the happiness of marriage and of life.

We have been given a unity which does not depend on

looks or on wealth, on health, on moods, or any physical intimacy which the years might shred and stale.

We know that God understands both of us and loves both of us more fully than we can ourselves. It is not God's plan that marriage shall be nagging, dull or tumultuous. His plan is for marriage to begin as a free joyful human relationship and for it to stay this way.

Doë and I have found from our personal experience that there is a full, instant and complete answer to every difficulty and problem of married life. Every single one.

It is available to-day, this moment, to the heart of each person willing to give God time to talk to them and to do what He says. It is as simple and as difficult as that.

No marriage is too far gone, no relationship too strained or sad or bitter for the superforce of a new spirit to restore it to freshness and serenity and life.

Folks who have complained in their hearts, and to their friends, of the shortcomings of their partners can to-day learn how to bring a change into their home instead of bearing a burden of discontent. They can substitute cure for criticism.

Many who have thought that the best of life was over have discovered a new youth and adventure to last them till they die.

In the old days Doë and I had a happy home. But we also had there, in greater or smaller degree, the elements of every situation which can destroy married happiness. No one can say where we might have finished.

Quarrels or disputes are now unknown things in our home. They just do not happen.

In the old days almost every day and certainly every week, things arose in our home, sometimes quite little things, on which we did not agree. Two people, however much in love, do not want the same things always all the time. One likes the wireless on, the other wants to read quietly. One wants to go to the cinema, the other doesn't. One likes a person that the other dislikes. One wants to spend the money of the family on something which the other regards as extravagant.

When a decision had to be made, I would often make it—and if it did not suit Doë, Doë would feel aggrieved. She became wistful and self-piteous.

At this point, from over my shoulder, Doë urges me to write that she used to become enraged and try to take it out of me in petty ways.

Often I would decide something first, act on my decision, and tell Doë of it after all was done. Then I would become grumpy and resentful if Doë were not enthusiastic. I would stay that way for a day or so "to bring Doë to her senses." "I'll show her," I thought. So Doë was forced to the place where for the sake of peace and progress she had to pretend an enthusiasm which was not always there.

All this time I was writing molten articles in the Press denouncing the methods of the dictators. But there was a dictatorship in my own castle. Yet so often I was blind to the fact.

In some homes the husband is the boss. In others the wife is the boss. And often it is a running and indecisive battle through the years relapsing into armed neutrality from time to time. Death sounds the "Cease Fire" and the result is a draw.

Yet there is a complete answer to conflict of will. It is to find a third will that both parties accept with enthusiasm. That is, God's will.

When I began to work this out with Doë in the home, it had an immediate effect on my office work.

In the old days if I had a grouch at breakfast, my whole department in Fleet Street was on the jump by lunch-time.

So, elsewhere, when Father suffers from an incendiary temper at home in the morning, by noon two thousand factory workers get hot under the collar and feel burned up inside.

The man who slams the door as he leaves the home is the man most likely to shut the door on negotiation round the conference table. The man who never says "I'm sorry" to wife or children will never break deadlock in industry.

The harmonies of "Music While You Work" do not remove memories of discord at breakfast and expectation of the jarring note at supper. Resentment, jealousy, instability and fear clog the mind and slow down the feet and hands.

> "No matter what the argument, no matter what the
>   fight,
> You never get a Jones to own he wasn't always
>   right.
> So when Dad was at the factory, he wasted hours
>   long
> While his mind held a post-mortem, working out
>   where Mum was wrong."

In the old days I often would leave home with a chip on my shoulder. I would be on the look-out for trouble— and find it without much difficulty. I would be sarcastic at the expense of my colleagues. I would fight for my own way, regardless of whether it was the right way or not. And my articles showed more spleen than usual when Doë and I got up against each other.

I found that in home life honest apology was the high road to honest peace. I did not see why, if it worked in the home, it should not work on the job. So I tried it at the office.

My first office apology had a detonating effect. In Fleet Street, when something goes wrong, the usual procedure is to try and fasten the blame on somebody else. But after my experience in the home I decided that when I made a mistake or lost my temper, or gossiped behind somebody's back, I would say the simple word "Sorry".

My office relationships were transformed by it. My work improved, because my judgment was no longer swayed by my feelings. I began to be a centre of sanity instead of a storm-centre. I found the simple truth that a man who has a happy home works best in journalism, or industry or anywhere at all.

The lessons learned with Doë, as we battled together to build a sound home, began to affect the lives of others with whom I worked.

What are the things which rasp and grate a marriage? I believe that dishonesty is one of them. I used to be a man who informed his friends that he could tell his wife anything. But somehow I did not do it.

Evasions and excuses—I would not call them lies. I told myself each time that my real object was to armour and preserve Doë's feelings. But they were designed to preserve the picture of me which I wanted Doë to have. It was love of Peter, not of Doë, which drove me on.

A mask in the home, even if it is only a small mask, even if it is transparent, if others know all about it and laugh at it, is a destroying and desolating force.

When I began to get honest at home about my own mistakes, I found it could become as much of a habit as dishonesty. I got honest at the office, and in my articles too. Whereas I would have written anything for the sake of a story beforehand, there were now certain things I would not write, even if it suited the convenience of the *Express* for me to do so.

Also I began to take a more careful view of my expense sheet each week.

How many homes are wrecked by money?

We had more than enough money for our needs in my *Express* days. Yet whenever Doë asked me for money I pulled a wry face. My object was to curb any extravagance in Doë by making it a difficult business for her to get her fingers on the cash. But in fact I was, and still am by nature, the extravagant one.

I would cheerfully spend £5 entertaining friends to dinner and drink at a restaurant. I enjoyed doing it. But I would grudge Doë an extra 10s. on her housekeeping money for necessary household expenditure.

One birthday I gave Doë a television set which cost £50. I always was keen on television.

Doë regarded this as a piece of extravagance. She would have preferred a present which cost less and was of more use to her. But she dared not tell me so, fearing I should be hurt and indignant. And indeed I should have been.

Nowadays Doë and I have learned to regard any money or property which comes our way as entrusted to us by God. We are its stewards and one day must render our account of it.

There is no longer any dispute between us as to how money shall be spent.

We reach a united mind before it is spent. When I found at home an answer to greed for money and to petty meanness alternating with silly extravagance, it altered perspective on my newspaper job and my whole life. Until then ambition and a desire for a bigger salary had been the fuel of my living. Now, for the first time, I was able to think of work and of life in terms of how much I could put into it rather than how much I was getting out of it.

The question of sex disturbs and destroys many homes.

Marriages based on a demand by one party or another for things which do not last.

Wives who have and love children and yet are left with a hatred of everything to do with sex.

Husbands and wives who pass a lifetime in the same homes and rooms together, yet never dare to tell each other exactly what they feel on this matter.

Wives who are resentful of their husbands, yet ashamed to speak of their resentment.

Husbands who are disappointed in their wives, yet make much of them.

So many young people enter marriage believing that in some way it will be the end of all physical problems. I did so myself.

Yet so many marriages are the beginning of new physical problems. It is a myth to imagine that a wedding ceremony transforms a hog into a gazelle.

Marriage should be a sacrament, not a mere source of physical satisfaction.

Doë and I both know that a unity and a freedom and an understanding beyond any human expectation is available to those ready to seek and follow God's plan, not their own, in every detail of their lives.

Children both before and after arrival can be a destructive influence, a dividing influence in the home. There is the fear of having them. I was always a little afraid of becoming the father of children. In my case it was fear of expense and that the children would cut across my own pleasure which squatted on my shoulders.

Doë wanted children. Yet she had a fear that the bearing of children would ruin her figure and sap her youth.

We know now that there is no need for parents so to bind themselves with fear. There is a superforce which offers the complete answer for such fears. Children are God's gift, not man's achievement. God will guide those whose joy it is to become the parents of children.

I was by no means enthusiastic when I began the experiment of trying, with Doë, to find God's purpose for every single decision of our married life.

But the truth is that it does work. All the poverty of strain and nervous ill-humour have been taken out of our home. Instead we have in it all the riches of a single-hearted and undivided mind.

Sometimes it happens that we have to do difficult things. God's plan for our home does not always fit exactly our human desires.

Yet I can say this. Never once since Doë and I decided to start our stony golden journey, have we been asked to do a difficult thing without being given the power and means to do it. However little we may understand God's orders, they always turn out in the end to be the wise and right ones. He knows better than we do the way to happiness. He knows facts which are not in our possession when He speaks to us.

He wants every home in Britain to become a sound home, a place of warmth and radiance and enduring happiness. A centre from which selfless citizens are turned out to build in office, farm and factory, a strong and united nation.

For it is the plan of God that homes made new shall be a prime weapon in bringing about the new world.

Doë and I have experienced much to uplift the heart in these last years. But the greatest joy has been to have a share together with our children in the reconstruction of the future, to feel part of a mighty and growing army advancing on a world front to usher in the new age.

Chapter XV

BRINGING UP FATHER

WHAT have Doë and I found in our new home? Happiness? Yes—but more than that.

We have had the joyful experience of rebirth. Our eyes were opened. We saw that our home, with all its comfort, its wealth, and the love and laughter of the good days, had become a fifth column centre in the war of ideas. It had been invaded by the enemy forces.

For, in spite of our success and worldly advances, we had let into our home many of those elements which undermine the character of a nation.

Now we have found new standards and a fighting quality. We have seen that we and our children have a front line place in the daily battle to build a sound nation.

What do I want for my children? A few years ago I should have said that I wanted the boys to be successful and the girl to marry well. Being by nature something of a snob, I should have been pleased to see my children going up in the world, both socially and financially. I would have wanted them to make names for themselves if they could, always to have an assured and if possible a substantial income.

Those were the things I put first when I considered the future of my children. If I thought of their characters at all, I took them for granted. I imagined that good character was something which just automatically happened to children who were brought up in a home with a father like me. That is a common belief in an age where "a character" has come to mean someone a little bit awkward or funny.

To-day I long to give my children character before all other things in life. I want them to grow up blade-straight, with nothing in their lives to hide, fearing nothing in this world but God, never deviating their speech or conduct by a particle in order to please men or from fear of what men may think or say, brave with the final bravery which prefers virtue to approval.

Cost what it may, I want them to do the right thing when they see it—and always to try to see it. I long for them to be pure in heart, so that their strength is as the strength of ten.

I pray that they may grow up into men and women who have conquered fear, irritability and the critical spirit, and who know how to pass their victory on to others. Also that they will have many people in their lives more important to live for than themselves.

Quality and character are the things I hunger to give to my children. For now I know these things are of more importance than security or success on the human level.

In any case they are the only security in the world to-day. Quality and character are good currency whatever the post-war world or future holds. Of what else can this be claimed?

In the old days my friends used to say of me, "Peter is such a fine father. He does love the children and is so good with them."

When I was in the mood, especially if visitors were in the house and it was important for the children to be on their best behaviour, I would romp with them and enjoy doing it. But if the children were naughty, ill, or noisy, if they coughed, howled, slammed doors or wanted me to tell them a story while I wished to read a book myself, if in fact they did the things children have a way of doing, I became peevish.

Indeed it was uglier than that. Sometimes I became angry.

It is true that I loved my children. I knew what it was to return home at the end of a day tired and pre-occupied and to have my heart warmed and lifted by the shouts and rushing welcome of Philip and Anne and Anthony. I knew, too, the wonder and content which creeps into your heart as, arm and arm with a beloved wife, you stand last thing at night breathless above the cots of your children and watch them draw their soft deep breaths of sleep.

Yet in the bad days my dealings with them varied between gusts of irritation and temper followed by gouts of sentimentality and slop to make up. The fact was that often I found my children a nuisance. I would not openly admit it. But that was the case.

My technique of correction was to bribe them with promises of treats, and to bully them by threats of penalties. "Now, Anne, I was going to give you a chocolate. But I shan't be able to do it until you stop that awful howling noise." "Anthony, run and get my slippers, there's a good boy, I'd be so grateful and I'll have a surprise for you when you have done it." "Philip, I'm not going to have you banging the floor with that hammer. It's absolutely intolerable and will give your mother a headache—if you do it once more you go straight to bed."

In fact, my efforts to induce the children to conform their conduct to my desires varied between a whack and a wheedle. Whether the whack or the wheedle was employed depended entirely on the mood of the billy-goat, not the conduct of the kids.

There are three of them, as you have heard. All are brown-eyed and tough-chinned. Philip, the eldest, is eleven. He has plenty between his ears besides skin, bone and hair. He gives his heart. He is a beloved companion, chattering away, eager to take a full part in every conversation.

He has, like his father, a nice sense of whether he is doing well or badly. And, like his father, he is a little too eager for the success and a bit too dashed by failure.

Philip finds it harder to tell his troubles than the other two.

Anne and Anthony both brandish their troubles in the air like clubs. When something is wrong they rush to find an audience to bludgeon.

Anne, aged eight, balances determination with diplomacy. If she falls down, she looks around to see whether there is someone who will come to her aid. If nobody is watching, she goes ahead with whatever she is doing. But if someone is watching, Anne considers whether she will begin to bawl. Sometimes she decides to do so. But as her mouth opens with the yells, both eyes widen also. If she sees her screams are ineffective, she turns off the tap. She can stop screaming as readily as a grown-up can stop talking. Like some grown-ups, she doesn't always choose to do it.

She is a loving girl. She shows more agitation over her brothers' troubles than over her own.

Anthony, aged seven, is the monkey of a Simian bunch. He has qualities of stickability. The older children run faster than he does. But he often catches them in the end. He goes on and on and on. They get bored. He continues.

He loves new clothes. It is a real misery to wear the same muddy playshirt two days following.

He has a sense of fun, mischief and revenge. The other day I reproved him for leaving the bathroom full of dirt. After several moments' thought he pointed his finger at me and said with a grin, "I'll put worms in your bed."

That evening I saw him carrying with breathless care a jar full of wriggling creatures. "Tadpoles will do," he muttered darkly to me.

Our children are no angels, Doë's and mine. They break the dishes, spill food on the tablecloth, tear clothes, yell and bawl, run across the flower-beds and lose scissors like most children. In fact, like their father and mother, they make mistakes, and are sometimes self-piteous and bad-tempered. That is the legacy they have inherited from us. Yet to-day Doë and I can say that our children in the home are a joy and a challenge to us, a cementing and reinforcing element in the household.

After we began our new journey all together, these thoughts which I wrote down came to me about my children.

"You always want the children to behave to suit you. But do you always behave so as to suit other people? Do you ever behave to suit them? You are not even ready to stop reading a newspaper if the children want to talk or play with you. You are full of worry and indignation if they tell you lies. Do you always tell the truth? You will not get them or anyone else to do what you will not do yourself."

To-day I have discovered that if I am willing to be honest with my children, they will be honest with me. It is as simple as that. Children, as they grow up, do what their parents do, not what their parents tell them to do.

How can parents who have never learned to say *No* to their own desires teach children to say *No* to theirs— even if they try? Instead, nowadays, some parents can only obtain obedience by force. The result is that in many homes the dictator mentality dominates as effectively as the dictators' sway has dominated the continent of Europe.

With other parents appeasement begins in the home. They yield to their child for the sake of a quiet life. So a young dictator is created—and the very quiet the parents thought they would obtain is lost. For the demands of all dictators are insatiable.

The forces of Materialism cash in on this tendency. In education and literature they urge "freedom", "self-expression" and "natural development" for young people. By it they mean young people should follow their own desires and be ruled by them. So the children rebel, and you get revolutionary situations in thousands of homes throughout the country.

Moral standards—the divinely-given guides to living, proved through the ages—should not be enjoined upon the modern child by parents, so the forces of Materialism declare. The child must arrive at these truths unaided and uninfluenced by the wisdom of his elders. Needless to say he shows small signs of arriving.

He moves off with gathering speed in the opposite direction. This suits the book of the militant Materialists. That is the sort of world they uphold as the end of humanity. The end it will surely be.

The Materialists have manœuvred us into the belief that the only alternatives of conduct in dealing with children are the Victorian idea of dictatorship in the home and repression, or the modern idea of revolt in the home and self-expression.

These are false alternatives. The third way is development under God by parents and children together as a family.

To-day I have discovered that if I take off my mask in the home, if I no longer pretend to be the wonderful creature I used to hope my children would think me, if I tell them quite simply of my own mistakes, they tell me of theirs. Together we find an answer.

The children do not pile up week after week their fears, feelings and reactions until you discover one morning that your child has a problem.

In the evenings we sit together, Doë and I and the children, and ask God to tell us what sort of a day we have had and how to make to-morrow a better day. We write down the thoughts which come to us and share them with each other.

So the children are learning an inner discipline, self-imposed, and they accept the parents' discipline when they know it is disinterested, based on God's will, not self-will.

The other day Anthony quarrelled with Philip. In the evening he put in his book, "I must not get tempered with Philip. Let us have a better day to-morrow and no battles." Then he went and kissed his brother and told him he was sorry.

Philip wrote, "Give Anthony back his soldiers." He told Doë and myself that he had persuaded Anthony a few days before that a box of new toy soldiers which he had been given were not so good as some old battered soldiers Philip offered him in exchange, and Philip had taken the new ones for himself.

A year or two ago Anne and Anthony had big battles with fear. When bedtime came they were scared of being left by themselves, and Doë or I had to sit with them.

So we began to pray all together about these fears. And soon the fears vanished.

Then some of Hitler's secret weapons began to soar over Suffolk. At night-time there were occasional bumps and rattles. And a window or two flew out of our farm. Many of the children in the neighbourhood became alarmed, and one of them, son of a farm-worker, came to stay with us. His fears were almost uncontrollable.

He shared a room with Anne and Anthony. After dark buzzing began and presently an explosion rattled the house.

The little child, aged 5, began to cry. Anthony, 7, and Anne, 8, both comforted him. They told him how they used to be frightened but were not any more, because Jesus was looking after them. Anthony wisely said, "It's gone off bang now, so there's nothing to be frightened of."

Then the two children prayed with him and for him. It was moving to see how, so long as they were thinking of helping somebody else, they had no fears for themselves.

We hear much talk of education nowadays. Is not this true education? To give children the secret of development and a sense of destiny?

To put them in touch with the power which changes human nature, and controls the universe?

To teach them how to be truthful, how to take a decision and stick to it, how to conquer fear, to confront difficulties in the spirit of cure, to get on with awkward and angular people, to direct natural emotions into healthy channels?

"All thy children shall be taught of the Lord, and great shall be the peace of thy children." That is the forgotten factor in all this talk of education nowadays. It is the basic education. Without it education lacks quality, and a mere increase of quantity may prove to be just more of a bad thing.

Children to-day have a date with destiny. They cannot escape it. History will record how they keep it. The "Isms" recognise this. They battle for youth. They have their propagandists placed in hundreds of British schools; they work through the cinemas and innumerable clubs. Homes would be the natural place to combat these alien ideas, but children of this age no longer have the home as the focus of their lives. The great majority of teachers still believe in sound values. But not all of them have a faith and enthusiasm for their right ideas to match the fire of the storm troops of the "Isms".

But all over the world the programme of M R A is providing young people with a sense of destiny. From many lands I receive the message of hope—tales of a growing and marching force of boys and girls who are united in a supreme programme to last them until they die.

I see this programme worked out daily by thousands of children in Great Britain alone.

Through it they grow up with a sense of their own responsibility for the future. It is a programme big enough to grip them, to launch them cleanly and vigorously into life.

These children accept the adventure of pioneering the future they will inherit. They have the spirit of true patriots—a lively sense that they belong to the nation and have a distinctive contribution to make to the life of the nation.

These young people of to-day, citizens of to-morrow, have a fighting faith which millions of us lacked in those years between the two wars.

CHAPTER XVI

BATTLE FOR CONTROL

DURING my years in the Black Street of Ink, I often visited the Black Valleys, where coal is mined to warm the industrial heart of our nation and make it beat.

Sometimes, in the Black Valleys, a sullen, muffled sound, like the subterranean hammer-blow of a giant, vibrates through the air and makes the earth quiver. For a moment every soul in the valley is still, heads cocked on one side, spirits suddenly swept to a pitch of apprehension, listening, listening.

Then the cry goes up, "Something's wrong down below." Out of every cottage the womenfolk come at the run, their heads and shoulders cowled in grey shawls, and away to the pithead. Sometimes they wait days there until the last still figure is carried up from below and there is no hope for the others crushed or cut off from the daylight by millions of tons of rock and scree and earth.

It was in the Valleys that I first saw how women take on men's countenances when they are in grief—then the taut, still, chiselled lines of the women's faces have a masculine appearance. The shape of one such face is etched for ever in my memory, the lips slightly parted, bitterness fighting faith in the deep lights of the eyes, the cheeks and chin soaking wet though no rain had fallen.

Class means nothing and hatreds mean nothing and the old political cries and slogans mean nothing at the pithead on days like these. Manager's wife and miner's wife brew tea together, stamping to keep warm on the blackened mud around the shaft. It is a sisterhood of sorrow.

Men from pit-face and office who for years have not spoken about each other except in terms of abuse, go down together to face the trouble—they work until clothes, hands and nails are torn. Sometimes they die in company, taking risks to cut their way swiftly to the entombed men. It is a brotherhood of travail.

Danger, as well as grief, brings out that quality of selflessness and love in man which is not always apparent in normal times. I remember one night in London when the blitz was at its height. For weeks on end, night after night the Germans had been over the city, smashing, burning, destroying. A sullen, dogged resolve to see it through, because no other course of interest or of honour lay before us, had gripped the citizens of London. But they were dark and desperate days.

Once late at night, I began to grope my way through the blacked-out streets to keep an urgent newspaper appointment. I was wearing a steel helmet which was necessary protection against the falling fragments of our own barrage. Every now and again I crouched in the corner of some doorway and flattened myself against a wall as the whistle of a bomb gave me a few seconds' warning before the jar and debris of the explosion.

Suddenly, travelling much too fast for safety, a taxi came careering along the roadway. It screeched to a stop. I noticed that its roof had two mattresses strapped on it, to catch any shell fragments that fell. The driver shouted to me, "Going my way, mate?"

In I hopped. He took me to my destination. In the black-out we overshot it.

The driver turned his cab around, climbed out and helped me with his torch to find the place I was looking for.

I asked him how much I owed him. He refused any payment. "I was on my way home anyway, mate," he said, and with a grin and a wave drove off into the darkness. I have never seen him since.

It was the same spirit I met in an immense factory. For several days Doë and I, on our Suffolk farm, had heard the sound of distant explosions. They were the signals of one of the biggest events of military history, the allied evacuation of Europe at Dunkirk.

Then I was asked to visit a factory where some of the machines most vital to Britain's safety at that time were being produced. There had been much trouble in this industry, with strikes and constant hatred and bitterness. The official who showed me round said, "Most of our people work overtime now without being asked. For the only time in my experience some of the men are working to finish the job without claiming payment, so we have to make special enquiries each week to see they get what is due to them. Our maximum production schedule is being exceeded by almost fifty per cent."

Sad that it seems to need the bad times to bring out the best in man. For, paradoxically, failure to bring out the best in man makes the bad times inevitable. And, in spite of the danger and uncertainty and anxiety of those days, were we not happier? Do you remember the comradeship and zest which sprang up among us in those dark hours and created a classless society overnight as all gave all for the nation? For a time we knew the joy and liberty which comes to the spirit of men when concern for ourselves is merged and lost in concern for our fellows.

How can we establish and extend this spirit in the post-war age? If we fail to do so, we shall assuredly lose the peace.

Already in Industry extreme interests of both Right

and Left are massing their forces and manoeuvring against each other. They are preparing to make Industry a battlefield as soon as the war of arms is over.

Their battle line of peace will be a battle for control. Management will fight to control Labour. Labour will fight to control Management. Government may attempt to control both.

Within the ranks of Management itself the battle will be on. Will counsels of progress or of reaction prevail? One big employer of labour said in my hearing the other day, "Don't worry about labour troubles. When normal returns, we can deal with them with our own weapons." By normal he meant unemployment at the million mark and over as a constant threat to every working man.

The Materialists of the Right treat labour as a commodity to be taken on and thrown off as convenient. They treat employees as ciphers in a ledger, as things not people. Some of them want to swing Management into a full-scale class war, to coerce and hold down the working classes. They want a class war for just the same reason as extremists of the Left—because they think they can win it.

Other employers, men of integrity, treat their employees well and are loved by them. Some see and fight the war of ideas. Others are proud of their paternalism. They cannot understand the criticism that paternalism is a drug to mask the symptoms of a diseased system; that it is a local anaesthetic, not a radical cure.

Yet they too bear a share of responsibility in the present situation. They are like men who are busy planning to paint their own cabins while the ship is sinking. There were some good employers in Russia before the revolution. They got on splendidly with their work people, and paid them good wages. But that did not bring the revolution of change which their nation desperately needed, nor, incidentally, when the revolution of blood came, did it save them. They remained part of a state of affairs which had to change. They failed to see or to fight the war of ideas. They had no plan big enough to remake the age they lived in.

Management has a key part to play in remaking the age we live in. The community needs its experience and cannot find that elsewhere. But it will be Management which is neither reactionary nor paternalist but revolutionary. That is, Management which has an entirely fresh conception of the function of industry.

"We are in industry for what we can get out of it" is reactionary and wrong. "We are in industry for what we can give mankind" is revolutionary and right. It is an approach which may mean fewer dividends for the few but will mean more happiness for the many.

A new spirit in the hearts of the industrialists would swiftly put industry at the service of mankind. And the first function of industry is service. It is to warm, feed, house and clothe the masses of the world. When the so-called captains of industry and indeed all who are involved in industry take the same responsibility for serving mankind as they take for the provision of their own family, we shall stand on the threshold of a new age.

Industrialists who still think in terms of sectional gain and self-interest are out of date.

It is this type of inferior thinking which plays into the hands of the extremists of the Left, men who preach class war and hope to obtain promotion in it. They are out for power. They bid intelligently for it. To them a grievance is something to be exploited for its own sake, rather than something to be put right for the sake of those who suffer from it.

Often those who advocate class warfare have a far

more vivid picture of the destiny of the workers than some of the Labour leaders of to-day. They offer the workers red blood instead of a blue print.

Within the ranks of Labour, two sections struggle for mastery. Shall extremists there, who love an alien ideology more than their own country, control the men who wish to maintain and recreate the best traditions of Trade Unionism? Or shall they be controlled by them? The sound elements in Labour are baffled by the subversive forces. They do not realise exactly what their game is, except that they do not like it. They do not recognise the war of ideas, and so they risk defeat in it. Many of them lack absolute standards of faith or conduct with which to measure the proposals and dealings of the Materialists—and when they apply the mere test of expediency, they find that, though they may not like it, the plan of the class-war boys is usually more expedient than their own. They discover that you cannot cure a passion with a mere programme. You cannot turn back passion by political manœuvres or a plain rebuke.

It takes a passion to cure a passion, a plan to beat a plan. Sound Labour needs an ideology and faith to answer the faith and ideology of the extremists. It needs fighters who see the war of ideas clearly and will fight as fearlessly, intelligently and publicly on one side as the extremists on the other. Otherwise sound Labour will go under.

The British Labour Movement sprang from Christianity. Faith gave it the fiery conviction of its early appeal.

The old Socialists had a philosophy which prevented them from lining up with class hatred and the use of armed revolution. They had a positive picture of free Labour in a God-controlled world. It was a super-national ideal. So advocates of class warfare found it difficult to make much headway.

Keir Hardie was the prophet of the revolutionary programme of traditional Socialism. His challenge to Labour was the same as Labour's challenge to society —the unselfish living and thinking which alone can finally outlaw greed and hate and fear. "Selfishness," he wrote in 1903, "is not by any means a monopoly of the rich. The same causes which lead the rich employer to lower wages or the rich landlord to raise rents operate quite as freely with working men when opportunity and self-interest dictate a like course."

He scorned the conception of the class war. "It is," he said, "a degradation of the Socialist Movement to drag it down to the mere level of a struggle for supremacy between two contending factions." His appeal was not to the material interests of one class but to the moral conscience of the whole nation.

The Carpenter of Nazareth and not Karl Marx was the inspiration of this great-hearted revolutionary, this champion of the oppressed.

So it was with the Tolpuddle Martyrs, the men who in 1834 were sent to Botany Bay for their efforts to establish an Agricultural Union and whose fighting faith was an inspiration to millions who followed.

From prison they sent out their battle-cry:

> "God is our guide. No swords we draw,
> We kindle not war's battle fires.
> By reason, union, justice, law,
> We claim the birthright of our sires."

Now British Labour has, in a large degree, cut its root, its fighting faith. The fruit has gone too. It was this to which Ben Tillett referred when on his deathbed he said, "The Trade Union Movement should stand for more than wages and sordid commercialism. It must develop a soul if it is to do its job of uplifting humanity."

With the rebirth of that spirit from which it sprang, the British Labour Movement will far outshine its past. It can become to-morrow more than it ever was yesterday. Labour led by God can remake the world.

Over the next quarter century Labour will have opportunities of governing great nations. Already the most farsighted elements in Labour are beginning to make their biggest contribution to the nation by bringing statesmanship into industry.

Men like these are recognising the greatest need of industry to-day. It is to clarify the true battle line. Men must come to see that they have been falsely and skilfully aligned on a front which is not the real front, so they are losing the real battle all the time.

The real battle line in industry is not between Labour and Management, where some would draw it. It is not between Left and Right, where others draw it.

It is between the constructive forces of Left and Right, Labour and Management, together on the one side, and the unpatriotic forces of selfishness in both that make for division and conflict on the other.

If Labour and Management will work together they can win this fight. Neither can do it alone.[1]

[1] Senator Truman, for four years Chairman of the Senate War Investigating Committee and, at the time of writing, Vice-President elect of the United States, addressing twelve hundred representatives of Labour and Management at Philadelphia on November 19th, 1943, spoke of the achievements of Moral Re-Armament workers in this field. "There is not a single industrial bottleneck I can think of," he said, "which could not be broken in a matter of weeks if this crowd were given the green light to go full steam ahead. . . . The time is ripe for an appeal not to self-interest, but to the hunger for great living that lies deep in every man. What Americans really want is not a promise of getting something for nothing, but a chance to give everything for something great. . . . We need this spirit in industry. We need it in the nation. For if America doesn't catch this spirit, we will be lucky to win the war, and certain to lose the peace."

As teamwork in the service of the nation is pioneered by constructive elements in industry, so teamwork will grow between the nations which industry serves.

For when sections within a nation, both Management and Labour, approach industry with the tiger mind of "What can we grab for ourselves?" that tiger mentality is carried to international trade conferences. So we have breakdowns which affect the lives of every individual in the world.

But with a new approach international conferences can become not a battle for markets but an alliance for service. When all plan for all to be adequately housed, warmed, fed and clothed, trade will cease to divide the United Nations but instead will unite the world.

In this new spirit lies our one and only hope of winning the peace and securing it for our children.

Men of courage in many countries have taken up the struggle.

Cecil Morrison of Ottawa, for example, is typical of thousands of employers.

He baked the King's birthday cake when King George and Queen Elizabeth visited Canada in 1939. His friends call him the "Happy Baker."

But Morrison was not always happy. His life was poisoned by hatred of everyone who interfered with him, especially competitors and organised Labour. Once in Saskatchewan he broke a strike. Subsequently he lost his business by his strong-arm methods, and when later, in Ottawa, he discovered two men trying to organise his plant for a bakery union, he sacked them.

The Canadian Congress of Labour took up the case. Mosher, its President, protested to the Minister of Labour. Morrison decided to brazen it out, saying that the men were laid off because of slack times and that their union activities had nothing to do with it.

Just then Morrison began to see that he was fighting on the wrong side in the war of ideas. He decided he must beat Materialism in himself, before he could help build sound industry. He asked God what he could do —and as a result not only re-instated the two men and paid them a month's back salary, but wrote and told Mosher and the Minister of Labour the true facts. By return of post he received this letter from the Canadian Congress of Labour, "May I say that in thirty years' experience in the Labour Movement, I have never known any employer do such a fine thing as you have done. If the spirit you have shown in adjusting this matter could be applied to industry generally, this world would become a very different place."

To-day the Happy Baker is fighting together with many Labour leaders, to bring that spirit to the whole of Canadian Industry.

Morrison has meanwhile had the opportunity of making a national demonstration in his industry. In September 1939 he united the bakeries of the Dominion under a National Council and gave them the aim of keeping the price of bread at its pre-war level. The Council demonstrated such a universal will to co-operate and economise that the Canadian Government repealed certain taxation on flour to assist them in their aim. They also appointed Morrison Administrator of Bread and Bakery Products for the Dominion. The overall cost of living in Canada has to date risen eighteen per cent since war started. The cost of bread ingredients has risen twenty-six per cent, and labour costs twenty per cent. But the price of bread has not risen one farthing.

In Britain two young Trade Unionists offer a first-rate example of industrial statesmanship by the ordinary man who sees the battle line clearly.

E

In the area where they work the bitterness between the men's leader and the manager of a large-scale concern had created difficulty and deadlock. At a critical period of World War Number 2 the men's leader called a strike which might involve 5,000 families. Work stopped.

The two young Trade Unionists talked things over. Then they called on the men's leader and asked him to come and see the manager with them. He said, "Not me. I'm not going to crawl to that you-can-guess-what."

The two young men then went to the manager's house. They asked him to write to the men's leader inviting him up to his house. The manager refused.

Then these two young fellows said something like this:—"Look here, sir, this bad feeling causes endless suffering. It must stop. Why don't you take the first step?"

After two hours' talk the manager pocketed his pride and they got their letter. The men's leader was so astonished at its friendly tone that he pocketed his pride and went with them. After several hours' conference every personal difficulty was ended. A provisional settlement, agreed unanimously by the employees in the morning, was drafted. The men went back to work.

The manager agreed to meet the men's leader face to face once a month and try to reach with him, in a spirit of honesty, the right answer to all problems arising in the undertakings within his control. From that moment a new spirit began to grow. Grievances which for years had rankled started to move towards solution. So every family connected with those huge concerns and the nation's interests also were safeguarded by the industrial statesmanship of two ordinary working Trade Unionists.

These two young fellows are out to fight the war of ideas throughout industry. They are out to build teamwork in the best interests of the nation and in the spirit of Keir Hardie and the Labour pioneers.

Chapter XVII

PEN INTO PLOUGH

INDUSTRY is in my breath, blood and bones. It is in my heart. Fleet Street and farming, the new and the old, the modern and the ancient of human craftsmanship and industry—my life is woven into the fabric of both.

Some men have beaten their swords into ploughshares and their spears into pruning hooks. I, for my part, exchanged my typewriter for a tractor. This is how it happened.

The Street of the Black Craft is either a graveyard or a granary for young men. They come a cropper there or else they reap a crop. Luckily my sheaves were golden. With inky fingers, greedily, I harvested the grain.

Then a crisis in my affairs arose.

I decided to write a book setting out the truth about the Oxford Group. I asked permission from the *Express* to publish this book. The answer I got was one which the *Express* was legally entitled to make—namely, that I could write a book on any other subject I chose, but not on the subject of the Oxford Group. If I wanted to write about that, I should have to leave the *Express*.

It was a big decision to make. But there was that in me which said that publication of the truth about a great world movement was of more importance than the fate of one journalist, even a journalist so important to myself as me. So, with regret, I picked my hat off the peg and said *au revoir* to Fleet Street.

I wrote and published my book. It is called *Innocent Men*. Its sales swiftly rose above six figures. It still sells

steadily, four years after publication, in Britain and many
other parts of the world.

And I hope it will go on selling.

I feel no sense of diffidence in recommending *Innocent
Men*. For I take no royalties from it.

.   .   .   .   .

Meanwhile, I was out of a job. I climbed into a
railway carriage and travelled to Suffolk. For I meant
to farm the land.

Doë and I owned a ramshackle old farm. We had
bought it in a fit of enthusiasm, and often afterwards
thought it was a mad thing to have done.

We had a romantic idea that the stream of money which
for so long in Britain had poured from the land into
the cities should be diverted back to the countryside
again.

We were earning plenty of money at that time. We
had a deep-rooted and sincere love of the land which
probably sprang from generations of farming ancestors.
Also we had an idealised vision of ourselves at the age
of fifty strolling, retired and happy, round our acres, while
the wind sent leisurely waves rolling across the cornland,
the summer scents and sounds drowsily arose and our men
loaded the clover-ley like fragrant tobacco into tumbrils.
So we bought our farm.

Much of it was in a tumbledown state. The hedges
marched out across the headlands and were tall with
years of neglected growth. The fields were hungry, and
in some cases starving. The land was hilly and awkward.
The ditches were full and many of the drains blocked.

But there was an atmosphere of vanished glory about
the place, a glory which had disappeared from so many
British farms and holdings during a get-rich-quick age
which despised and neglected agriculture, a glory which
could be restored.

The farm-house had the shadow of old nobility about it, though many of the rooms were covered with layer upon layer of garish wall-paper, concealing the oaken beams beneath.

The pinnacle of the barn roof towered up like a cathedral into the dimness, heavy with the memory of master-crops from harvests long since garnered and rich with the hope of huge, cool, yielding heaps of grain in years to come. The fields, thirsty for the hoof of cattle and the sweat of man, lay patterned to the rain and sunshine expecting rich and fertile days.

Our farmer friends told us that it would take five years before the place could be made to pay. But at that time my salary from the *Express* came rolling in. Doë and I did not see any reason why it should ever stop. Indeed, such an idea never occurred to us. So we bought the farm and expected to spend £1,000 a year on it for several years.

Now suddenly our whole circumstances had altered. My job and salary had vanished overnight. I knew a little of the theory but next to nothing of the practice of farming.

There is a big difference between a man in a highly-paid job in Fleet Street who owns a farm and has plenty of money to spend on it, and an ex-journalist with an old farm which is losing money fast and which is the only means of livelihood for himself and his wife and children.

As I travelled eastward towards Suffolk in the corner of my third class carriage, I felt the prickle of fear. I was up against the timeless, ageless, endless problem of man—how to wrest a living from the stubborn womb of the earth. Would the land be my master or my servant? Would the old farm break me or would I break it? I knew one of these two things had to happen.

But coupled with these same fears was a feeling of exhilaration and resolve. Now it was hammer and tongs, back to the wall, neck or nothing. It was boots and all, with boats and bridges burned.

I had a sense of pioneering. For I knew that when war was over, with the immense complications and upheavals of national economy which would inevitably follow, thousands of city dwellers and ex-servicemen would turn their minds and step toward the soil.

If I, with my slick city mind, so unsuited to the age-old processes of nature, and with my soft city heart and hands, so bare before the rugged character of the land, could make a go of it, many would tread that trail with new confidence and hope.

On our first evening in our old farm-house, Doë and I talked these things over together. We decided to farm for the country, not for ourselves. That is, not to treat the land as a kind of cash box and beat and bang the last penny out of it for ourselves, but to treat it as a national asset to meet national need, to be stewarded and served and improved so that we should hand on to the future better than we had received from the past. We took to ourselves the old farmers' saying, "Live as though you would die to-night. Farm as though you would live for ever."

We decided that in every farm decision, as in every other decision of our lives, we would do our utmost to find God's will and to carry it through.

So we sat late together, Doë and I, in the old farm-house kitchen which had weathered the storms of four hundred winters, which had heard the tiny sounds of birth to usher in each new generation and later had seen it die, which had sheltered the laughters and tragedies, the tears and dreams and voices of countless unknown yeomen of the past, our predecessors in the place, and would haven the hopes and fears of many more through the centuries after we in our turn were forgotten.

We knelt and prayed together, that first night in our old farm-house. It was a habit we had lost in the clatter and drive of Fleet Street, but which seemed both natural and necessary in the quiet midnight of our farm bedroom at the beginning of our new adventure.

So many romantic pictures of farm life a townsman has—white geese with a bare-armed, brown-skinned girl feeding them from a bowl, long lazy days with forks amid the shocks of corn, great log fires in the winter-time with chestnuts on the hob, after a hot bath following the long day over root and stubble with a gun.

But townsmen forget the other side of the ledger— cold, wet, endless mornings when you strain your inside out cranking a tractor as the pale dawn breaks—then doggedly sit for hours on end bathed in the oil fumes and the damp mizzle which blows in from the North Sea.

Days when the dust from the thrashing tackle inflames your eyes until they are red as a ferret's, while the sharp barley havils work their way through your clothing and grate the skin. Days of mud and fatigue, of sweat and chill and damp—many days of hardship and disappoint- ment before the inevitable annual miracle of the harvest.

Man's battle with the soil is endless. The very moment he ceases to grip and drive and master it, the land begins its silent, swift retreat back to the jungle. It is spiritual as well as physical warfare. For the earth is a living thing. It grapples with a man. Its resistance chal- lenges the deep resilience and steadfastness of the human spirit. The old East Anglian farmers knew what they were saying with their proverb "Break a field—and make a man."

So many memories of those early days of our farming

adventure come crowding in upon me—and most of them are of Doë.

She had lived all her life in cities. Her clothes and hats often came from Paris, which was the European capital she knew best. Her hair was curled and cosseted, her nails a delicate and almost human shade of pink.

She dreaded life in the country. She was afraid it would turn her into a vegetable. This made her clear conviction about the rightness of our decision with the *Express* even more compelling.

Life on the farm drew forth from its scabbard, where Fleet Street life had laid it, all the shining, unconquerable steel of Doë's spirit.

I see her now, sweat dripping off her brow on to the baking summer earth, hoeing, hoeing, hoeing until the time came for her to prepare the evening meal.

I see her in an old mackintosh, with a sack tied round her head and shoulders, her body bent forward like an arrow against the horizontal December rain, rescuing hens from swamped hen-coops and bringing home a handful of eggs triumphantly for our winter meal.

I see her standing upright with one hand rubbing her aching back and the other sweeping away the hair which had fallen into her eyes. She had been chopping and laying hedges, blackthorn, elm and crab, which for twenty-five years had felt no slashes upon them. Before her on the iron-hard frosty winter earth a huge fire burns up the branches of the hedge. The ash of the fire has blackened her face, except where the sweat makes white patterns from her forehead to her chin, and where her eyes, full of laughter, shine out.

Best I remember her in the evenings, when the day's work was done, when new difficulties had to be faced and planned, when sometimes it seemed hard to continue, to know whether we should pull through, when the temptation was to sell the place at a profit, which we could have done, and to get clear.

Doë never faltered. She saw steady, cool and straight from the beginning. She had the dauntlessness of heart and the confidence in God which makes it hard for others to keep secret their fears or to maintain them.

To-day Doë's hands are chipped, chapped and stained. Yet they are lovelier to me than in the days of expensive and fragrant manicures in the West End of London—lovelier in the sense of more to be beloved. For they are the hands of a mature spirit which has stood full stature through the grey days. She has fought and triumphed in the battle of adversity.

Day by day, week by week, month by month we planned, toiled and sweated. So many mistakes we made—but we wasted none of them. We learned from each one. We hacked the hedges and dug out the drains and ditches.

We smashed down the stubborn pan of earth with steam-ploughs and deep-cultivators.

Patiently we plodded behind the horses as their massive limbs pounded the soil like pistons, their breasts cleaving the frosty air before them.

We bought cattle, and last thing at night travelled with lanterns round the darkling yards, feeling the warm breathing of the beasts upon us and hearing the age-old rustling as they plunged knee-deep in the straw.

We hacked and hoed and harvested. As the huge roots thudded into the bottom of the tumbrils in the autumn with a sound of thunder, we felt the reluctant earth slowly, stubbornly begin to budge before our efforts.

.   .   .   .   .

Suffolk has the sense of eternal values about it. It is part of the great invasion belt of British history. Danes,

Romans, Normans, Dutch, all these and many more have swept over East Anglia and left traces of habit and language behind them.

As the plough breaks the soil there, it may turn up flint weapons, coins, pottery, skulls and bones. Sometimes a whole Viking ship is dug up. It was dragged inshore and buried with honour and feasting centuries ago after its days of pirating and adventure were ended.

Our village was a centre of the wool trade in Edward III's reign, and our house and barn are built of timbers from a ship which sailed the seas in the days of John Cabot and the seventh Henry. Perhaps it was one of the little ships which repulsed the Armada under Drake. Down the road in our valley Cromwell marched with his Ironsides, the russet-coated, round-headed East Anglian yeomen who farmed these fields—and it was from these counties that the Pilgrim Fathers gathered to sail out in the *Mayflower* to a new world.

In Suffolk they talk a sing-song, delightful dialect which Doë and I found hard to understand when first we went there. "Bardsnazun" is Suffolk for birdsnesting. "Meesen" means mice and a "four-a-lete" is a crossroad. They call an awkward girl a "Slammakin" and a "hornipie" is a curlew.

I was astonished when, soon after we bought the farm, a villager said to me, "Master, du ye let I make a Titter ma Tatter for yer boy." He meant to ask if he could build a see-saw for my son Philip.

Another one described a local tradesman to me as a "stingy article", by which he meant an ill-tempered, queer customer.

Two days after Christmas I and one of my men took sixty rabbits to market. The dealer who bought them had enjoyed his breakfast, and it had plainly been of the liquid variety. My farm man wrinkled up his nose at the strong, beery smell which surrounded the dealer. As we turned away he clutched my arm in great excitement and cried, "Du ye get that, master? *Cor, 'e pong like an ole ferrut, 'e du.*"

Doë and I had been told that we should be treated by the Suffolk folk as foreigners and strangers. Instead, we found welcome and warmth.

For the Suffolk farmers and villagers, when they discovered that Doë and I were aware of our own shortcomings as agriculturalists, and were eager to learn, took us to their hearts and invited us into their homes. They made available for us a wealth of experience and instinct and wisdom which only uninterrupted generations upon the soil can supply.

Our farm men gave us a friendship and loyalty which warmed our hearts.

Our neighbours offered us advice when we asked for it, help when we needed it.

When our barn was empty of food for stock in the first lean years, they sent us sacks of supplies. When we needed implements they lent them, and often supplied men to drive them too. Ungrudgingly and with a generous spirit they helped us onward in our attack upon the soil.

In return we were able to offer them the new spirit of our own home and lives, and a fresh philosophy for British agriculture—that it may be part of the destiny of the country folk of Britain to fill the hearts of the nation with new faith and fire, as well as to fill larders with food.

The Government was appealing for farmers to employ women labour. So we took on and trained eight landgirls. They live in the farm-house with us. One used to be a cutter in a London store. Another was a cook.

Another used to work in an office as secretary, and one used to appear on the stage.

So many people, with differing ages, tastes, backgrounds and temperaments—it offered a first-rate chance of learning to live together and like it—the secret which men and nations have forgotten.

A depth of unity, understanding and appreciation grew steadily among us, by change not by chance, as together we battled to make the spirit of the new Britain we were fighting for come to birth in our own house.

We began to hammer out together a five-point farm philosophy, to meet the needs of the age. Here it is:

1. *"What can I do for this land of England?"* not "What can this land of England do for me?"

2. *Grow character as well as crops.* We try to make each other better people as we work together to make a better farm. We found that living to make the other fellow great as you work alongside him holds the secret of teamwork and of happiness, and answers the bitterness of industry.

The land calls for qualities of endurance. It has no use for those who quail before difficult situations and difficult people. It demands the stickability and faith we need if we are to preserve and extend our heritage.

3. *Democracy works when God is the boss.* We decided that every big decision, whether about farm or household policy, should be taken unitedly in the heart of the family on the basis of discovering *what* was right, rather than *who* was right. Often one of the land-girls would be given the distinctive idea which saved time and money, or which developed new advances of character for the family.

4. *When God guides, He provides.* We have put to the test and proved the age-old truth that those who are willing to go to God for orders are always given the

material things, manpower, time and money, necessary to obey them.

5. *If you put your heart into your work, you find it puts heart into you.* There is much hard and unpleasant work connected with the land. We have found that it is not what we are doing or how much we are getting out of it or where we are working which makes us happy on a job. We are happy at any job if we give our best to it— and discontented if we do not.

To-day our farm men and their families, as well as farmers and workers of surrounding farms, are with us on this programme.

There is an old story of the hermit who discovered the secret of happiness—and, though he lived in the remotest forest of the uttermost country in Asia, the world carved a highway to his door. When Doë and I bought our Suffolk farm, we chose the spot partly because it was so remote. We wanted to get away from people. In the last three years over one thousand people from every part of Britain have visited us at our farm. During the last twelve months alone over four hundred names appear in our visitors' book—and they do not include the scores of folk who drop in just for a meal or for the day.

We have our guests sleeping in tents and the barn during the summer. One man wrote to me, "Your home, which began as a country retreat, has become a national advance."

Members of Parliament, Servicemen, miners, dockers, industrialists, Trade Unionists, parents and children, Americans, Australians, Canadians, editors, the high and the low, the rich and the poor all pass through our doorway, and many take something new away with them as they go.

Each year we hold a Horkey. Horkeys are hundreds of years old. They are the celebrations which in old days farmers and men with their families held in their barns each year. All broke bread and thanked God together for the harvest.

From East Anglia the Pilgrim Fathers gathered to sail. In 1620 they made their landfall in the West. In 1621 their first harvest was safely in, and with memories of the barns and villages of East Anglia, now for ever left behind them, they held a Horkey.

So Thanksgiving began. And while in America this festival of family and earth has been maintained and enriched, in England we have let it die out.

We hold our Horkey in the barn. Its oak beams and rafters have that dark silver glow, merging into gold when the shadows fall. In the bays are tons of beans and oats, shot in great heaps on the floor—food for the cattle in the months ahead.

The walls are decorated with red berries, leaves, huge sheaves, globed golden mangolds and long, tapering sugar-beet, white against the oak, with its vivid green foliage, like parted tresses above it.

At long trestle tables sit our guests, one hundred and sixty this year, American soldiers, Government officials, Trade Unionists, newspapermen, folk of every kind from many parts of Britain, and our farmer friends, farm workers, land-girls, thatcher, blacksmith and harvest hands.

The atmosphere of harvest seems to give everybody an appetite. Home-cured ham, bred, fattened, killed and cured on the farm, mashed potatoes, salad, apple fool and rolls go fast down the red lane. Iced fruit cup, cream cheese and scarlet apples fill in the crannies.

Then there are songs, recitations and speeches. Most years the local blacksmith gives us a recitation and our horseman plays a trombone solo.

At our last Horkey our Member of Parliament said,

"If the spirit and teamwork of this farm as I have seen it can spread throughout the nation—and it is doing so —it can solve every problem of the strenuous days ahead. It can be done, it should be done and it must be done. I promise you to-night to work to make it so in this constituency and at Westminster."

But the tribute which perhaps gave greatest joy to our landworkers and ourselves came from an old man of eighty-six who walks slowly up and down the only level stretch of road in our neighbourhood, because it tires him overmuch to walk uphill. Seventy-eight years ago he began to work as a boy at Hill Farm. The farmer then was the famous Sam Hustler, who was known far and wide for his success in mastering the soil.

This old chap said to one of my employees, "When Mr. Howard came to the farm, nobody thought he'd do no good there. It was a poor old place, and awkward to farm. It was badly let go. But I watched he, so I did. And soon I says 'There's another Sammy 'Ustler up a-there'. They all laughed at me, but it was true, sure enough. Look at yer crops to-day."

Certainly the old farm has responded generously to what we have done together. In the last three harvests, our number of stacks has risen from nine to twenty-three, and in the interval we have bought an elevator which builds bigger stacks to-day than we did at first.

We grew a year's sugar ration for three thousand six hundred people last year—most of it off land which had been written off as useless. We were told, "Don't sow anything there. You won't even get your seed back."

There were no hens or cows when we arrived. Last year we produced fourteen thousand eggs. We have a growing herd of T.T. cattle. Last year we produced thirteen thousand gallons of milk for the nation.

When first we came to the farm, Doë and I and our

landworkers wrote a poem giving our vision of what we saw for the farm.   Part of the poem ran like this:

"Now, under God, we guardians of the soil
Dedicate all we have in toil and prayer,
Not for the swift return in cash and kind,
But recreating craft in husbandry,
And stewardship and quiet sufficiency.
So both our cottages and farms shall know
The multitudinous fruitage of the soil.
The barns shall sag and tremble with the corn
Beam-high, rich pyramids of warmth and gold.
Broad stallions, thunderous hooved, shall pace the earth
And fertilise the pastures.   While the cows
Wax fat and richly yield in calf and cream.
Huge hogs shall grunt and snore away their time,
While bees garner the honey murmurously.
We, stewards of the Hill, plan under God
To shape this farm to perfect purposes,
Perfect in every detail, so to mould
This message to the nation and the world."

Our vision is now on the way to becoming true.   But it is not through anything we of ourselves have done. Indeed we are people who began with small agricultural knowledge and with no idea of how to work out an answer to the needs of the age.   Yet it is a fact, proved by daily renewed experience, that God does guide all those who listen to Him, and acts when they obey.

This is the basis of our living at the farm, and the years have proved that it stands the test.

Chapter XVIII

DESTINY OF SERVICE

ONE-QUARTER the population of the globe.
One-quarter the land surface of the earth.

That is the British Empire. What are we to make of it?

Mr. Churchill announced, "I did not become His Majesty's First Minister in order to preside over the dissolution of the British Empire."

But the waxing and waning of empires are governed by forces more cosmic than the words or even the decisions of men who occupy the seats of human greatness at one time or the next.

The imponderable and immeasurable spiritual force which surrounds and controls this universe has stretched out its hand from the unseen to lift man's empires up, and then to cast them down again, according as they have served or disobeyed its purposes.

.   .   .   .   .

I got a first-hand impression of the British Commonwealth of Nations from Indians. They came to Brighton in the last war to recover from their wounds. They were given, as hospital, the pavilion which George IV built. He used it for cards, wine and women. With the help of Mrs. FitzHerbert, Lady Hertford, Sheridan and Fox, he turned the fishing village into a society den.

More than a hundred years later in Gentleman George's pavilion, the smell of disinfectant and disease was substituted for the scent of powder and port wine.

The Indians bore terrible wounds. Some had lost both legs. Some had both arms blasted away. They were pushed around in the bath-chairs which before that War had taken rich dyspeptics for their daily ventilation.

They were brave and kind men, those Indians. Their keen faces were patient under pain. They used to smile and talk with me, and wave as they were wheeled by.

It was gossip in Brighton that religion forbade one or two of them the use of anæsthetics and antiseptics. So they faced operations conscious and unafraid and later had sea-water baths to heal their stumps and scars.

Whether this rumour was true or false, it coloured my childhood picture of India. I thought of Indians as the embodiment of human endurance and chivalry. I grew to love them.

Canada, too, is a part of the Empire which runs in my blood. My great-grandmother, Sarah Howard, cut her ties with Europe. She crossed the Atlantic in a small wooden sailing-ship, taking her children with her. She settled in the "blue-nose" coastal belt, near Halifax, Nova Scotia. And she educated her children there by sacrifice and sweat.

She passed on to them her rugged and obstinate quality.

Two of my mother's family emigrated to Australia. From them tales came back of huge sheep ranches, of days spent on horseback and of camp-fires and billy-can tea.

One of my ancestors had been with Livingstone in Africa. My grandmother passed on to me an old letter received from him, with a dark stain on the envelope which I told myself was blood.

I pictured the blackness and heat of the sudden tropical night, with hostile natives, silent and uncanny as jungle beasts, creeping towards the encampment where Livingstone and his companions were sleeping.

Inside the tents, Livingstone and his friends were armed, not with guns or grenades, but only with the weapons of integrity and the sword of the spirit to conquer the Dark Continent.

I had a vivid and warm conception of the British Empire, as I grew to manhood. It was almost a family affair, and something which no other people throughout history had been able to build in the same way.

I was proud of the British Empire. It meant something personal to me. I had a stake in it. I meant to go and look at it one day. And I was stirred by the conception of millions of unknown men and women, who never had seen me and whom I never should see, united by the spirit of a common loyalty which was stronger than party, treaties or agreements.

The British Empire stood to me for adventure, toughness and character.

I saw the Commonwealth of Nations rich in gold, copper, pearls, iron, coal, rubber, and cattle, rich in the variety of its tongues, colours and races, standing as a mighty world force for good against evil.

I thought the British Empire was the embodiment of the best things British character stood for—selfless courage, square dealing, equality to all men, help to the underdog and freedom for the oppressed.

As I grew into manhood my views changed. My conceptions of Empire were debunked. Some of the cleverest men I knew, and whom I greatly admired, laughed as loudly at the out-of-date idea that the Empire was something to be proud of, as at the out-of-date idea that faithfulness in a home was the done thing.

People who accept and propagate this view, intellectuals who lightly discard the great fact of the Empire without ever considering what its true destiny should be, are merely the dupes and tools of the destructive forces of Materialism. But I did not see this at the time. I did not recognise the war of ideas or realise how decisive a factor in that war an Empire dedicated under God to the service of man could be.

I met self-styled Imperialists. A certain type among them were gross, self-satisfied and self-indulgent. Their countenances were mottled by overdoses of alcohol and their lungs corroded by overdoses of nicotine. They regarded themselves as Empire-builders, but seemed more like those who reap the gain of other men's labours.

As I grew up I was told by my intellectual friends that the Empire was merely a cash proposition. We had grabbed it by force. We were in it for what we could get out of it. It was something we ought to be slightly ashamed of. Interest and enthusiasm were definitely not the thing.

I was told that Colonel Blimp represented my idea of the Empire. Certainly Colonel Blimp, as portrayed by the cartoonist who sired him, was a farcical figure. He appeared most days in the Press arrayed in a bath towel. He had a silly face. Also the things he was given to say were as foolish as possible. He was proud of the Empire, which he spelt "Empah", and this pride was portrayed as one of the most ridiculous things about him.

I looked at Blimp. I laughed at him. I did not want to be thought like him.

When I met certain men from the Empire, I had to face the fact that my old conception of a happy family of nations was shaken. Many of these men were not bound by the same loyalties as myself. Some looked eagerly forward to the day when their countries would break the bonds of Empire, as they expressed it. They were critical of the way they had been treated. They felt they had had a raw deal.

I lost interest in the Empire. It became rather a bore. So did those who wished to discuss it.

      •   •   •   •   •

Then I went to work for Lord Beaverbrook. For a long time he would discuss nothing but the Empire. And he certainly was not a bore. He was as boring as a wagon-load of guncotton in a match factory.

I suppose Lord Beaverbrook is one of the greatest living Imperialists. His enemies may say that reflects on the modern conception of Imperialism. Just the same, Lord Beaverbrook is a man with a vision. Like or dislike him, love or loathe his policies, he is one of the few public figures who were not ashamed to keep men's minds fixed on the Empire throughout the inter-war years.

I have seen him spring from a sunbath in his private garden near Leatherhead, to prance about the grass delivering a twenty-minute oration on the subject of the Crown Colonies. Then he sinks back on his couch, glares at me for a moment, says, "For God's sake, Peter, when will you learn not to address me as if I were a public meeting?" and roars with laughter.

I have heard him talk about the Empire while shaving, while sitting in the dentist's chair, while having his hair cut, and with his mouth full of continental food prepared by his Alsatian chef. He talks about it in French trains and German liners, in pyjamas and dress clothes, in season and out of season.

For me and for millions, Lord Beaverbrook rekindled an interest in the British Empire. But something was missing. In spite of political campaigns, many of them outstandingly successful, in favour of Empire Free Trade, the problem of India increased and increased. So did the problems of Newfoundland and Jamaica. The conflict between the French and English in Canada continued to grow nearer. The Dutch and the British still glared at each other in South Africa.

Lord Beaverbrook's policy said that Britain's interest lay in a closer economic unity within the Empire.

And while this may have been true, it neglected the eternal truth that if you represent an *interest* you inevitably divide people and arouse the opposition of all those who have other interests.

If you represent a *principle*, you rally the wise and honest to your standard.

It was sad and strange that Lord Beaverbrook's Empire programme had cash-appeal but lacked heart-appeal. For many who would have been stirred by the heart-appeal denounced the cash-appeal as selfish or ill-conceived.

What did Lord Beaverbrook's Imperial policies lack? They lacked the inspiration of a new factor which must enter in if the British Empire is to achieve its true destiny.

In India recently a statesman and scholar who is an understanding friend of Britain summed up what he felt was lacking in her administration. After paying a wholehearted tribute to the work of the British people in India, he concluded that in their manner of doing it they have proved "highly intelligent and immensely insensitive."

The same principle is illustrated by the true story of the English woman and the Burmese woman. The English woman said, "Why don't you like us? Look what we have given your country. We have given you railroads and radio, and newspapers and steamers and telegraph, and law and justice and protection."

The Burmese woman replied, "Yes, you certainly have. I am grateful for all these things. But have you given us your hearts?"

She did not mean slush and sentiment. She meant a relationship based on heartfelt equality and respect on both sides, a relationship of mutual caring and esteem by which the two races, side by side, could solve their problems together.

It is this lack in British administration which produces the paradox and tragedy. The British Civil Service have never administered our Imperial territories more honour-ably and ably than during the last twenty-five years, yet Britain has never been more unpopular in India and in some other places than to-day, nor has her rule been more questioned by democratic nations.

The bitterness has grown greatly in the last few years. In India you feel it in the shops, on the train, in the bus, everywhere. Indeed it has become so all-pervading that many Indians have now convinced themselves that their own deep centuries-old divisions are just a creation of British propaganda. They passionately resent the sug-gestion that before receiving political power they should put their own house in order. Yet, at inter-Indian conferences, each section presses its own demands and they fail utterly to reach agreement.

So India has met deadlock. And for the first time in the history of British rule something like despair is possessing the minds of wise British and Indian lovers of the great sub-continent.

Is there no hope? Is there no way to pick the lock of the deadlock?

In Simla, in 1944, an event took place which may be the beginning of the new India. It was little heralded by the world Press. But it was noted by the men of power and responsibility throughout the continent. Gandhi in his ashram heard of it. So did the Viceroy in his palace. News of it reached the grey-stoned India Office building in Westminster. It was hailed by one of the greatest living authorities on the Indian problem as "an event unparalleled in Indian history, indeed in any history."

This event immediately concerned Burma, the rich province which was secured to the British Crown by Lord

Randolph Churchill in 1886. It was an action taken by a minority, the Anglo-Burmans, the people of mixed British and Burmese blood. In the old Burma before the Japs came this minority had been intensely jealous of the privileges and safeguards accorded to it by the British Government. It felt these safeguards were the only bulwark against the Burmese majority, who resented the superiority they felt the Anglo-Burmans assumed towards them.

Now the leaders of the Anglo-Burmans, gathered in conference at Simla, recommended their community to give up all these safeguards and privileges. They wished in future "to consider themselves a people of Burma and to rely for their security on the confidence and friendship of the Burmese people."

Section after section of the Anglo-Burman community in India ratified this bold stand—the charter of an entire community on the "give" instead of on the "get."

Other Burmese communities were pricked to the heart. A Moslem barrister of the Court of Rangoon gave the reactions of the Indian minority in Burma. After stating that the Indians' attitude as a community and as individuals had on occasions been wrong, he said, "If all the ability and labour we Indians have shown in 'getting' is to be turned to 'giving,' Burma will regard her Indians as a precious asset."

The Indian barrister added, "I would like to see the Indian community voluntarily give up its claim to separate electorates and to special safeguards. If the motive of every community is to give rather than to get, who then would want any safeguards? Unless we can secure the confidence and goodwill of the Burmese people, paper safeguards can be nullified any day. Goodwill and friendship would be of greater and more lasting value than temporary economic advantages."

Another leader of the Indian minority, a Hindu head-master, commented, "We need to go into the new Burma to work for the welfare of Burma primarily and not for her exploitation. We need a new leadership of those who are prepared to serve, to give, to help, and not of those who want to amass, to hoard, and to carry back to India. 'How shall I make Burma great?' should be the question asked, not 'What shall my community gain?'"

Meanwhile the Karens, the largest minority of Burma, declared that in future they intended to work with the majority, which they had always preferred to avoid.

What was the Burmese reaction to all this? It is given in a remarkable document which has come into my hands, written by a man regarded as one of the leading Burmans of the day.

"I can conceive of no better contribution to the making of a Burma that works," this Burman states, "than what has been done by the Anglo-Burmans. A lead has been given by Burma to the world on the question of minority communities and it may well be that the Anglo-Burman Conference at Simla made not only a declaration but history. . . . My emotions at this change of heart evinced by two important minority communities of Burma were at first elation and gratitude. But these have now been followed by an overwhelming sense of responsibility. It will now be my privilege to evoke a true response from the Burmans and I have not the slightest doubt that the Burmans will respond in a like spirit of generosity and trust."

How did all this happen? What was the cause of this series of events in which many see the hope not only for a new Burma, but for a new India also?

The answer lies in the secret of change. These minority and majority leaders of Burma had met changed Englishmen walking about on two legs. These men were different from the usual idea of an Englishman.

For they had decided that the way to the heart of India's problem was a change of heart—starting with a change in themselves.

As soon as they began to change they proved the truth of the great Lord Sinha's advice to the Lloyd George War Cabinet: "Always remember Indians are the most responsive people on earth."

Indians, Burmans, Karens warmed to these men. Here were people they could say things to which they had never said to any Englishman. Here were people who not only believed in them but expected the best from them, who were concerned that all Britons should live to make the Burmans great. These English were not blind to the Burmans' need for change. Indeed, they saw right through them. But they had the insight to live the statesmanship of being the first to change.

There sprang up a new comradeship, a teamwork which introduced a new factor into the most insoluble of problems. The Burmans suddenly saw that the differences between communities could become not a cause of weakness and confusion, but a force to unite and enrich the nation.

What was true between Karens and Burmans, they now sensed could be true between Burmans and British. A leading Burmese nationalist wrote: "Whatever the future of Burma may be there will be room in it for the selfless Briton who comes to give of his best to her. In her path towards Dominion Status she will need the help of Great Britain; Burmans of intelligence give this tribute to Great Britain, 'If Burma must be under tutelage for a short period before attaining full self-government, she would rather be under British tutelage than any other tutelage, and when we have achieved our freedom, we would prefer to be an equal partner in the British Commonwealth of Nations than an independent country on our own.'"

So the simple conception of change is to-day producing the new statesmanship which cures imperial problems instead of merely shelving them or shovelling them out of sight. It offers a fresh alternative to the materialistic dilemma of "exploit or evacuate." It provides a third way to Indians faced by the equally materialistic dilemma "hate or submit." It solves the problem of relationships, and could change either staying or going, for both British and Indian, from tragedy into triumph.

Often the cold and superior attitude of some Britons makes the Indians unwilling to accept even the best things we in Britain have to give them.

This cold and superior attitude is felt not only by Indians, but by Australians, Canadians, New Zealanders, South Africans, men from the Colonies, and not less by Americans. It is the greatest single barrier to our working with anyone.

We call it "reserve" and are rather proud of it. Others look upon it as large-scale conceit. We find it hard to believe that other nations do not see us always as we see ourselves—the best, finest, truest people on earth.

Sometimes we think of ourselves as the Mother country. So we might remember the story of the wise mother who had a large family of children. If one of her children was troublesome, she gave him a dose of Epsom Salts. But on days when all of them seemed troublesome to her, she took the dose of Epsom Salts herself.

When the Mother Country gives a lead in the spirit of change, the response is immediate.

Sir Sikander Hyat Khan, when Premier of the Punjab, declared publicly that the spirit of change is the beacon light in a dark world. That M R A holds the only answer to the problems of India.

Mr. Curtin, Prime Minister of Australia, at the time when his country was threatened by a Japanese invasion, in a national broadcast called his people to re-arm morally as the surest foundation of national strength and urity for the tasks of war as well as of peace.

Lord Bennett, as Prime Minister of Canada, declared that the work of the Oxford Group in that Dominion made the task of government easier.

We need a change of heart in our approach to every Imperial problem—and many await solution.

There is the question of Australia's population—who is to fill those vast, empty spaces, if they are to be filled?

There is the question of New Zealand's isolation far from her friends and close to potential enemies.

There are innumerable problems, not least of them the fact that in the last few years and under the immense pressures of war many Colonies and Dominions have undergone the transformation which the Industrial Revolution brought to Britain—the change-over from an agricultural to a manufacturing community.

There are the racial questions of South Africa and Canada.

But India remains the key to our Empire's future. If, by a change of heart, we find solutions to the problems of that vast sub-continent, we shall find solutions for every other problem of Empire and world relationship.

India is recognised by the subversive forces of Materialism as the keystone of our whole Imperial edifice, so they concentrate the main strength of their divisive attacks upon it, endeavouring to stir up unrest between the various peoples of India and Britain.

Also they use their own version of British administration in India as a major lever in their efforts to separate the United States from Britain.

India is the link between East and West. Western

civilisation will be judged by the Eastern world in the future as in the past according to the success or failure of its regime in India. Also India offers the West the chance of learning all the lessons the Eastern world has to teach us, and which for generations we have been too proud to learn.

India may divide or unite the United Nations. With a new inspired philosophy of Empire, Britain can win the heart not only of India but of China, and the gratitude of the whole world. It is Britain's opportunity for greatness.

A new world will come about through a change of heart in men and nations. It will not happen any other way. And if Britain sets the pace of change, she will in a fresh and stirring way capture the hearts and imaginations, not only of the citizens of her own far-flung Dominions and Colonies, but also of many another land.

So the Commonwealth can become the pathfinder for the unity of the world. It can be a pattern for the unity of all free nations and go forward to fulfil a great destiny, with many friends, in the leadership of all mankind.

Speaking of this task, the Earl of Athlone said: "Throughout her long history this country never failed, and has not failed now, to meet recurrent crises with the courage which each demanded. But the spiritual crisis remains, and calls for action. Nation and Empire must stand or fall by our response to that call. The choice is moral re-armament or national decay. That choice will decide whether ours is ultimately to go the way of other dead kingdoms and empires, or whether our Commonwealth, led by God, may become a leader of the world towards sanity and peace."

Chapter XIX

THE HOUSE WITH A HOME INSIDE IT

IN Berkeley Square stands the house of miracles. Few who pass that grave, beautiful building know that inside its walls history is being made.

Massive with destiny, dappled with sunshine and shadow through the foliage of the giant plane trees (their luxuriant growth attributed by tradition to the fact that they are rooted in an ancient plague-pit), it gazes from the past into the future across the bustle and commotion of to-day's one-way traffic in the Square.

It was the home of one of the most successful Imperialists of all time. Clive of India bought it when he returned in triumph as victor of Plassey. The purple and panoply of human greatness were heavy upon him.

He decorated his new house with glittering ceilings, doors made from Brazil wood which he shipped from the East, and stone fire-places which still give expression to the inspired quality of the mind that conceived and the hands that moulded them.

But what did all his wealth achieve? Hounded by critics who resented his success both as conqueror and reformer, dulled by the drugs he took in increasing doses to ease the pain of his diseased frame, he went upstairs one winter afternoon in 1774. His family heard his footsteps pacing up and down, up and down. Suddenly there was a thud. They rushed in and found the great man dead upon the floor.

Some say he cut his throat. Others that he hanged himself. Others that he died from an overdose of opium, which he took in large quantities to numb his sufferings. But we shall never know the truth. His family said nothing. They smuggled his body away at night and buried it beneath a plain stone in the country.

For nearly two hundred years Clive's descendants lived in that stately home in Berkeley Square. Many strange and adventurous happenings took place. there. Behind its impassive walls kings, statesmen, fighting men and beautiful ladies intrigued, gossiped, dined, danced, did business, settled the affairs of nations, loved, wept and laughed.

From a green-panelled room on the ground floor the card-players arose in anger one winter night and in the corridor swords were drawn and honour satisfied with a deadly thrust and a still figure carried secretly away.

A few years ago, the ownership of this house changed hands. It was up for sale. And from many parts of the world men and women who had seen the march of Moral Re-Armament and recognised its destiny as a growing force in world affairs sent gifts to make Clive's historic house available as the headquarters of the work in Britain.

What goes on inside the house to-day? It has lost none of its beauty. But the thing which catches your breath as you enter is the warmth and spirit of the place. It is a house with a home inside it, a place where thousands of hearts move out to welcome you as you cross the threshold and where suddenly all the best ideals of your life, tarnished or perhaps forgotten in the rough and tumble of the years, take on a new lustre and seem worth fighting for again.

To-day Clive's home is the nerve centre of a new world order.

I first went there during the blitz. And I found the cellars, where Clive of India stored his beer, sherry, port and champagne, put to a new use. Neatly white-washed, equipped with double-decker bunks, they were the dormitories, dining-room, and offices of the most remarkable cross-section of the nation I ever had met.

Two champagne cellars were named the House of Lords and the House of Commons respectively, because members of these assemblies were accustomed to sleep there night by night. I found Service men and women, passing through London, who came to this home to equip themselves with a fighting faith to carry them into battle. There were Trade Unionists and industrialists, newspaper men and teachers, several families blitzed out of homes in the East End, admirals, generals, city workers.

It was a constantly shifting multitude, yet all felt at home. For it is a quality of Clive's house that it provides a setting in which people of every class and condition meet together without embarrassment.

A Cabinet Minister and a cabman can sit down together in the same room and neither of them feel out of water. I have seen this very thing happen there.

In the kitchens, where the old spits, equipped to roast whole animals, still hang, meals are cooked on modern stoves and served for the hundreds of people who pass through Clive's house daily.

As you can imagine, the wash-up is quite a business. It is an amazing thing, in this day and age, to see every evening mixed squads of male volunteers, who have done a hard day's work in factory and office, turn up, roll their sleeves and tackle the kitchen and scullery wash. All work wholeheartedly together, big business men alongside clergymen, shop stewards, bankers, bakers, Service men, Labour officials and fellows from the factory bench, and they teach each other plenty as they give this contribution. Housewives from every part of London give up a day a week from their own homes to contribute to the household duties at Berkeley Square.

The advance of the work is only made possible in

wartime by the passion and selfless service of these hundreds of ordinary men and women. It is a tragedy to see requests come in for help from industry, from the mines, from civic and educational authorities, requests which have to be refused. For the trained wholetime personnel of MRA, possibly the only people in the country with the experience to bring cure to situations which cost Britain tens of thousands of man hours and many men's lives, are engaged in other forms of National Service, scattered in response to the clamour of bigots and the zeal of venomous men who hate and fear all that MRA fights to establish. Nevertheless the story of MRA in war-time is a miracle of advance.

From every part of Britain and from men and women the world over who owe remade lives and homes to the new spirit come letters, parcels and contributions towards the material provision of the headquarters in Berkeley Square. The pioneers of Moral Re-Armament themselves have little money, but they have faith in the world they want to see, confidence in each other to share fully, holding nothing back, and a reliance on Divine Providence. These men and women hold all things in common, and believe that God will supply their material needs if they are guided by Him. They put this age-old truth to the test and it bears the proof of up-to-date experience.

The place where Clive fell dead is now the sleeping quarters of a bunch of young airmen. In the corridors where the duel ended fatally, food is now served from hotplates to guests in the rooms alongside.

The drawing-room where Clive received his guests, where generations of his descendants entertained their friends, where King George V of England was welcomed, is now a private theatre. In the last years and months I have seen leaders from every walk of national life and men at the head of Allied Governments sitting

F

in that place, and they have been given fresh hope and inspiration there.

The rooms of Clive's house are scenes of constant miracles and adventure. Day by day from every part of the country men come there with unsolved problems. Sometimes these problems affect their home life. Sometimes they affect their industries.

Sometimes those who come have problems of statesmanship to be settled, for many great men make their way like Nicodemus, secretly, to the place where they know an answer lies. They go away with fresh hope, with the solution to their problems offered to them, and with the certainty that their confidences are unbroken.

As you pass from room to room in the house of miracles, each place offers fresh surprises. I have seen men and women whose bodies and lives had been wrecked by years of strain and suffering receive new health and peace of heart in Berkeley Square.

You will find representatives from every section of some industry, Management, Labour and Government, sitting round a table to talk out their difficulties man to man in a spirit of openness and honesty together, and unitedly discover an answer. You will find groups of people planning to carry this new philosophy, sprung from age-old truth, to the millions and the leaders of the nation.

So many scenes to touch the heart crowd in upon my memory as I think of the last two years in Clive's house. I remember soldiers, sailors and airmen who prayed with me and with others before they said good-bye—and many never came back again.

I remember the night the miners arrived. They were the representatives of the men. They had come to London for a conference to settle the future of the industry. These were difficult days and the hands of the Press and the people were against them.

They came crowding through the front door, with the burr of Northumberland, the sing song of South Wales, the rolling consonants of Scotland and the broad vowels of Yorkshire in their voices. That night they caught a glimpse of the part they were meant to play in building a new world order. "The spirit here would solve every problem of the pits," said the leader of 100,000 men. And later we heard how many dark situations were illuminated by the vision these men took away with them.

We had the coal-owners too, some of them with granite faces and, it had been said, granite hearts. But somehow as the evening wore on, eyes twinkled, hearts warmed and granite melted. You saw then what industry could become, if men of goodwill on both sides of it started to fight together for a great programme of national service instead of fighting each other for sectional interest.

I remember during the Empire Conference when Prime Ministers and their wives, representatives of many of the Dominions and Colonies, accustomed to command and to be obeyed, were given by ordinary men speaking of their everyday experience a new picture of what a Commonwealth of Nations should be—how a sound family of nations begins with nations of sound families—and how they went away with their heads higher and with their shoulders set in an attitude of hope.

Best of all I remember Christmas evenings when the secret and spirit of the whole place is made plain. In the large entrance hall where Clive piled his teak trunks and packages of treasure on arrival from the East, a huge Christmas tree stands. One year it was given by friends among the workers at Covent Garden.

The tree is candle-lit. From its topmost branch a silver star looks down. Underneath the branches, in the straw-thatched crib, the Child lies by His Mother's knee in the warm candle-glow. Around them are the admiring shepherds, the wise men with their gifts.

And thronging the hall, lining the great staircase, hushed, breathless with wonder and love, the crowd stands. There are families from the dockland of the Thames and from Mayfair. There are statesmen and servants. There are Labour leaders and industrialists, bosses and workers. And there are scores and scores of children.

Presently, soft and beautiful, from the minstrel gallery high above, where the violins and sackbuts played vainly to soothe the anguish of Clive's heart, steals the old carol:

> "O little town of Bethlehem,
>   How still we see thee lie!
> Above thy deep and dreamless sleep
>   The silent stars go by.
> Yet in thy dark streets shineth
>   The everlasting light;
> The hopes and fears of all the years
>   Are met in thee to-night."

The crowd squats on the floor and joins in other favourites—"Nowell", "Come All Ye Faithful" and "Still the Night".

The shadows from the candles leap and flicker on the wall. They dance across the intent and eager faces—the faces of men, women and children from all classes of life and from all sections of the nation, warmed and united by the fire of the greatest idea ever given to mankind.

They are like-minded, and the future is theirs, a symbol and a sample of the new world to be.

The air is peopled with memories of the past and promise for the future. On such a night as this a new friend, visiting Clive's house for the first time, looked long into the centre of light, and murmured, "Is that what Christianity means? I never knew."

Chapter XX

WE NEED NEW MEN

YOU do not judge a nut by its shell. You do not value a jewel by its casket. And in the same way, the outside appearance of a man's head does not always reveal the quality of the interior—which is fortunate for some of us, and not so good for others.

When I was at Oxford University, often I saw two large feet, encased in shiny black crinkly boots, coming round the corner. Some distance after them the owner followed.

He was a strange-looking gentleman. His blue eyes peered out at the world, over a wispy grey beard, through thick-lensed spectacles which gave them the appearance of the headlamps of a motor-car.

Behind them was packed one of the finest pieces of mental machinery in the world at that time. For he was B. H. Streeter, Provost of the Queen's College, one of the most brilliant scholars of the age.

He had the charm and eccentricity of genius. His chief parlour trick was limericks. He used to invent them and recite them on the spur of the moment to suit any occasion. Always he stood on the towpath beside the Queen's College boat at the start of the bumping races, and encouraged with some epigram or wisecrack. Once when they were trying to catch a Corpus boat, he remarked—"Habeas Corpus"—and they did.

B. H. Streeter was a Doctor of Divinity. He was the leading authority on the Four Gospels. He wrote books on Philosophy, History, Comparative Religion, Psychology, Ethics and Mysticism. It has been said of him that he was almost the only British intellect in his field recognised as possessing the authority of genius by the professors of continental universities in the inter-war era.

He was at Oxford during the early days of struggle when Frank Buchman was at work there building up and training the leadership destined to carry the Oxford Group message all over the world. For years he watched the work grow. Finally, on July 11th, 1934, he rose to his feet at a public meeting in the Oxford Town Hall, and said, "My attitude towards this movement has been what diplomats call a benevolent neutrality. I now wish to say publicly that I ought to cease from an attitude of benevolent neutrality towards what I have come to believe is the most important religious movement of the day."

Three years later he wrote, "By 1934 I had seen enough of the Group to realise that it was making bad men good and good men better faster than any other movement, and I decided that it was my clear duty to step into the boat and handle an oar, instead of continuing to shout from the towpath a judicious mixture of criticism and encouragement."

Streeter sought speed. For with his insight and his knowledge of the trends of history he foresaw catastrophe unless a new spirit spread swiftly enough to plant changed motives of living in millions of human hearts. Working with the Group in Scandinavia, for the first time he realised that this change of heart can move with matchless speed, swift enough to outpace the oncoming forces of Materialism.

Streeter said: "Modern civilisation can only be saved by moral revival. But for this it would suffice if every tenth or every hundredth was changed. For each such person raises the level of those whom he touches in the home, in business, and in public affairs."

The first news I had of the developments in Scandinavia which gave B. H. Streeter hope was contained in a newspaper paragraph. I saw it in 1940, while I was still in Fleet Street. It said that Fredrik Ramm had been arrested by the Nazis.

I was interested because Freddie was a brother of the Black Craft. He was a Norwegian journalist, with an international reputation. He flew over the North Pole in an air-ship with Amundsen. He was a jolly, rollicking hulk of a man with a first-rate mind. He used to visit Fleet Street from time to time.

I made some enquiries about his arrest, and discovered an amazing story.

In October, 1934, C. J. Hambro, the President of the Norwegian Parliament, asked a hundred of his friends to meet him at an hotel outside Oslo. About a thousand turned up, and Freddie Ramm was among them. He travelled up to the mountain hotel with a young Englishman.

"What is going to happen up there?" Freddie asked. "Miracles—and you'll be one of them," was the reply.

It came true. For the meeting called by Stortingspresident Hambro at the hotel outside Oslo was the first meeting of the Oxford Group in Norway. It meant the start of a new journey for Freddie, which eventually led him to his death, as a result of the treatment he received in a Nazi concentration camp. But before that, it produced results which made the Norwegian Foreign Minister say, "When the truth is told, Ramm will go down in history as one of Norway's greatest heroes."

Describing four years later what happened to him at that hotel outside Oslo, Freddie said, "I told God—'If you exist, I am willing to let my life be run by you.' God began in me by extinguishing all hatred, all negativity, and all fear in my relations to other people, classes and nations, and just as if the miracle were four minutes

old and did not lie four years back in time, I remember
the liberation which came to me and how the ice in my
heart melted and a new and unknown feeling began
to grow, and a love of men unfettered by what they
could give me."

Freddie became a uniting instead of a divisive force
in Norway. He began in his own home asking his wife's
and children's forgiveness for the coldness of the years.

Next he turned to his old journalistic and political
enemies. His motto had been, "Strike first when you
suspect anybody of being an antagonist. Strike so hard
that he falls. Strike again so that he does not recover."
There was no love lost between the Conservative and the
Farmers' parties. Yet a year later Freddie, the Conservative, travelled to Denmark with Mellbye, the
founder and president of the Farmers' party, so that
both could heal their breach with the Danes.

This breach had arisen from a dispute over the his-
torical rights to Greenland which had been referred to
the Hague International Court and decided against
Norway. Freddie, with some friends, had so stirred up
hatred against Denmark in his newspaper columns that
there was danger of a deep rift between the two countries.

Now Freddie climbed on to a platform at Odense,
Hans Andersen's birthplace, and told three thousand
Danes that he was sorry for his hatred of their country
in the past which had now ended. It was Norway's
National Day, when the nation celebrates the anniversary
of its free constitution. This marks Norway's breakaway
from Denmark; yet Freddie, the Norwegian, asked his
audience to join with him in singing the Danish National
Anthem. There was a moment's hush and then without
a word of prompting from anyone those three thousand
Danes sprang to their feet and burst into the Norwegian
Anthem so the walls shook with the sound.

The impact of the Group in Norway itself was swift and decisive. The Group's idea caught the imagination of the youth, just then subjected to a bombardment of unexampled power from the "Isms" of Left and Right.

When the Group first arrived in the country the Rektor of Oslo University welcomed their influence, saying that the student body was being assailed by subversive moral and political forces and that he was powerless to stop them. In another great educational institution, the Institute of Technology at Trondheim, the student council had for seven years been dominated by Marxist elements and other political extremists.

The year after, Trondheim chose a student influenced by the Group to be president of their Students' Representative Council, and at the national Students' Conferences of 1935 and 1939 it was remarked in the Press that "the Oxford spirit" dominated the Conferences. So came true the words of four Oslo professors in 1934, in the London *Spectator*, "The coming of the Oxford Group will prove to be a turning point in Norwegian history. They have come at the strategic moment with the right answer." Who can estimate the effect of this new spirit in the heroic fight of students, professors and teachers when the Germans came?

Among other results achieved through the work of Ramm and his friends in the years before the outbreak of war with Hitler are the following. They bore out the view of President Roosevelt that there is no problem—social, political or economic—which would not melt like snow before the fire of a great spiritual awakening.

1. *Taxes.* A flow of conscience money, unofficially estimated at 7,000,000 Kroner in the first two years, began as a result of the application of the standard of absolute honesty in many lives. A Supreme Court Advocate, five years after the Group's coming to Norway,

stated that every fortnight since that time his office had been engaged in some conscience money case as a result of the Group's work.

2. *Morals*. *Arbeider Bladet* (The Daily Worker) and *Bymisjonaeren* (The City Missionary) remarked on the decrease in prostitution: "The demand has sunk because so many men found the secret of clean living and happy family life through the Oxford Group."

In 1937 the legitimate birthrate showed an upward tendency for the first time for thirty years. The President and Secretary of the Norwegian Midwives Union publicly attributed this to the rebuilding of sound family life through the Oxford Group.

As typical of many cases, a cashier in an Oslo bank voluntarily confessed to an embezzlement of Kr. 108,000 which had gone many years undetected—and announced that his action was due to the Oxford Group.

3. *Church*. Stortingspresident Hambro, writing in November 1944, stated that Frank Buchman was "the catalyst who made possible the united church front in Norway during this war."

Bishop Berggrav, since 1937 Primate of the Norwegian Church, was at that mountain hotel near Oslo with Freddie Ramm. He was a focus of attacks by Professor Hallesby, the head of the conservative and fundamentalist element. The two men did not love each other. The rift between them symbolised a split through the whole Church.

The day war broke out in Europe Berggrav, who like Freddie had learned that God can direct a man's thought, sat in his study. Suddenly, luminous and compelling, the thought came to him, "There is a war in Europe. There is also war between you and Hallesby. Go and see him and make peace for Norway's sake."

The Bishop was a big enough man to pocket his pride

and obey. From that simple action—coming as a climax to years of faithful and inspired work by the Oxford Group—sprang the fighting and unbreakable unity of the Norwegian churches, which were the admiration of the world, which were the spearhead of resistance against the Nazi invaders and frustrated them at every point during their occupation.

That is what Quisling, who had left the Communists to lead the Nazis in his own country, meant when he complained that "the whole soul of Norway had been poisoned by the Oxford Group," while Berggrav described the Oxford Group in Norway as "the most important event since the Reformation." So it is not surprising that the Oxford Group was banned. The reason given was that it was "part of the British Secret Service."[1]

Freddie was at the core of Norwegian resistance to the Nazis. He stood at attention and sang the Norwegian National Anthem as the Nazis marched through Oslo. He wrote a series of articles called "What to do in the Black-out." The Nazi censors thought they must be harmless with such a sensible title, and let them go through.

Then they tumbled to it and Freddie was arrested. He was put in a room with a rope across the middle of it. They offered him "golden freedom" if he would

---

[1] On this point Stortingspresident Hambro writes: "The Germans decreed in Norway that the Oxford Group was a part of the British Intelligence Service and should be harshly suppressed —a most flattering and slightly ridiculous compliment to the British Intelligence Service. The Gestapo feared and hated the Oxford Group as they could never fear and hate the British Intelligence Service. They hated them as men hate and fear the ideals they have lost and prostituted, the faith they have betrayed. They feared them because instinctively they knew that the Oxford Group was part of God's Intelligence Service preparing the way for an ultimate defeat of the principles of evil."

quit his religious convictions. He refused. Then a Gestapo chief came in. He said, "I am the prosecutor." He read out a list of charges. Then he hopped over the rope and said, "Now I am the judge"—and sentenced Freddie to death.

Later he was reprieved and sent to Hamburg. He was kept there two years, most of the time in solitary confinement. His rations were meagre. The Germans offered him more food and a measure of liberty if he would make munitions for them. He refused.

Finally he began to die. The Germans put him on a train to go back to Norway. As the train crossed the Danish frontier, a friend put a little Norwegian flag in his feeble hands. It stayed there till the train reached Odense, the scene of Freddie's great reconciliation with the Danes.

There Freddie died. His memorial is the impact of his work on the life of a nation. It will be seen in the years ahead.

Freddie well illustrates the leadership which this age demands. It did not rest in power or position, but in the power of change. The miracle in the mountains transformed him from a partisan into a patriot. He takes his place in history because he led in change. He saw, with the prophetic prescience that God gives, the needs of his nation, and by changing to meet them, pioneered a philosophy of greatness for the millions.

Another example of this new leadership is Pim van Doorn, a young Dutchman. He was a creature of fire, colour, life.

In 1937 he was an undergraduate of Leyden University and a leader of the student body, although he had interrupted his career to enlist with the Ethiopian army fighting the Italian invader and to join the French Foreign Legion.

He met the Oxford Group at the Dutch National Assembly in Utrecht Market Hall in May 1937. Later that year he sold what he had so that he and five other Dutchmen could take part in the Moral Re-Armament campaign in the Scandinavian countries.

When the Germans invaded Holland Pim was allowed to continue his studies at the University. But his fighting faith was more than a match for the alien ideas which the conquerors brought with them. He waited for his chance to join in the war of arms. Meanwhile he fought the battle of ideas every day.

When he graduated the Nazis ordered him to work in a munition factory or serve in their army. He determined to escape to England. With him in his pocket he took maps of all the airfields of Holland. But on his way to the little ship which was to take him to England he was captured. After a brief imprisonment he was shot. While he awaited execution Pim wrote the following letter to his father and friends:

"Looking back, I am extremely thankful for my life—above all to God for the way He has led it and has made me live magnificent things. I shall shortly be happier than you. Don't be sad, but rejoice in this grace. I pray that you may accept my departure in peace; that there may be no premature revolt; that I may not be a cause of sadness, but that strengthened by it you may all put your shoulders with greater devotion to the common task."

Pim's life and death is a symbol of the new spirit of youth which will make Europe rise again out of the ruins. His spirit, strong and without bitterness even in death, will march on in the hearts of thousands of his comrades and point the way to a Holland finer and greater than before.

This is the leadership of the future. It goes to ordinary

men empowered by the superforce of the Holy Spirit
to do extraordinary things.

Frank Buchman has said, "People believe that their
leaders should be guided by God. But the rank and file
must be guided too. A God-guided public opinion is
the strength of the leaders. This is the dictatorship of
the living spirit of God, which gives every man the
inner discipline he needs and the inner liberty he desires."

Anyone can be such a leader.

Recently there died in Philadelphia a little frail lady
of sixty-nine named Annie Jaeger. The news of her
death sent a tremor to the hearts of millions in every
corner of the globe. In castle, cottage and slum dwelling,
in countries she had never visited, people felt that they
had lost a leader and a friend.

Eleven hundred Londoners gathered in Canning Town
Public Hall, birthplace of the British Labour Movement,
to honour her. Leaders of London's East End boroughs,
which had taken the greatest weight of the blitz, said
that Annie's spirit had given them the courage they
needed, while a hundred families marched up to the
platform to announce that she had brought them unity,
love and purpose where there had been distrust and drift
before.

The Stockholm Press gave this little lady a two-column
obituary. The news agencies flashed the story of her
life to papers in all parts of the free world, and messages
of sympathy for her son were smuggled out of the occupied
countries into Switzerland and Sweden. At her funeral
she was carried up the aisle by representative leaders of
labour, while 260 American Labour newspapers mourned
this "Mother of British and American Labour."

A typical American comment was, "Rugged steel-
workers in Sweden, thousands among the now 'silent

people' of Europe, members of Parliament at Westminster, civic leaders throughout East London, workers in the Lockheed and Boeing aircraft works, men in Washington, employers and organisers, soldiers and civilians with their wives and children will mourn the passing of a fearless prophet and true friend. Annie Jaeger was a great and gracious lady, with as big a heart and as fighting a spirit as any that her native England has ever sent to these shores."

Who was Annie Jaeger? A woman born to power, riches or distinction? A woman educated from youth for the task she performed so well?

She was none of these things. At sixty she was a little widow who kept a small shop in Stockport, Cheshire, and worked day and night to earn a living for herself and her only son. Her health was indifferent and everyone took for granted that her life was doomed to run along the same groove until the day of her death.

But the new spirit gripped her. It made her sell her shop and leave her home.

It armed her with its miracle-working power and set her tramping from home to home, from labour leader to industrialist, in London, Scandinavia, America, wherever it led her.

It transformed her and turned her into a national and international statesman—a prototype of the statesmanship of the future.

Chapter XXI

HOW TO GET IT

HOW to get in touch with the superforce, the super-passion, the super-wisdom of a new spirit and make it real in our own lives? That is the question many ask.

It takes me back to that luncheon in the Temple, where I first made contact with this dynamic power myself.

At that time talk about God was to me just a bore. I felt freer and easier without it. The most amusing and intelligent people I knew were not interested in it. Most of them had no belief in God. Nor had I.

So, proud and gay, I strode forward to meet the adventure of my life. The earth was my goblet and I planned to drain it dry.

That day at luncheon in the Temple, my neighbour told me he believed in God.

I told him I did not.

He asked me "Why not?"

For some reason, I found it difficult (I, so slick of the tongue that I could hold my own with Cabinet Ministers) to provide a cogent answer to that simple enquiry.

I swallowed a mouthful of food to take time for reflection. Then I said to him, "Well, why do you believe in Him?"

This man replied, "It is as foolish to argue about whether there is a God as it is to stand looking at an electric-light switch and arguing whether if you turn it the light will go on. One fellow says it will. The other says it will not. The end of the argument is to turn the switch and see."

I asked this man what he meant. He told me that the way to see whether God was there was to put Him to the proof. He declared that God would talk to each person who was ready to listen and obey.

I said this sounded far-fetched to me. But as I looked at this man, I knew he believed what he told me. He was living at a swifter pace than I, and he had in his eyes a peace I longed for but never had grasped.

When I told him again that I did not believe in God, he smiled and said, "In that case, you won't mind listening to Him, will you? For you won't expect to hear anything anyway."

He suggested to me that, as an experiment, I should take four separate sheets of paper. Then write at the head of each sheet one of the four absolute standards Christ preached in His sermon on the Mount—Absolute Honesty, Absolute Purity, Absolute Unselfishness and Absolute Love. And that I should ask God to show me where I fell short of them and to write down, holding nothing back, the thoughts God gave me about myself on each of these Four Standards.

"You may think the thoughts God gives you are ordinary thoughts," he said to me, "but be honest about them."

And he told me the story of the countryman. This old fellow, it seems, had a conscience that troubled him. At last he went to a farmer and said, "Master, I'm sorry. I stole a rope from you a while back." His master forgave him and the countryman went away. But he still had no peace of mind. For he had not told the farmer that there was a cow at the end of the rope when he stole it.

I was living in my club in Northumberland Avenue at the time. Next morning, in a cynical spirit, curious but without belief, I sat up in bed and made the experiment this man suggested.

Do you remember the tale of the small errand boy who stood outside the Tradesmen's Entrance? On it was a notice: "Beware of the Dog." The small boy said loudly to himself several times, "There ain't nothin' there. Garn, I tell you, there ain't nothin' there."

Then, looking cheerful and cocky, he walked through the door.

But he lost the seat of his breeches just the same.

.   .   .   .   .

I walked through the gate not believing God was there. That did not affect His situation in the slightest.

On that morning in my club God spoke to me, as He speaks to every person who is not too proud to listen to Him.

At that moment my mind was illuminated. I began to see the truth—the sort of man I was, the sort of man God wanted me to be.

Some of the things I wrote I had known deep down in me for a long time, and had taken care to keep them in the depths if they showed signs of coming to the surface. Others I had never suspected.

But here is the amazing part of the affair. Some of the things I wrote down that morning on those sheets of paper were habits, both of thought and deed and word, which I had known for a long time were wrong. Yet I enjoyed them.

From time to time I had taken a resolution to cut one or another of them out of my life—and after a day or so they returned. Now God told me they had to end. And I knew I could not do it.

I went to meet the man who had spoken to me at luncheon in the Temple. I told him where I stood.

He said to me, "God will transform your nature— but only if you let Him. If you put right all you can put right, God will put right the rest."

He said I must take the simple decision whether I would let God run my life for me or not. He added in matter-of-fact tones that it was like a transfer of property—that if I meant to do it, I had better tell God so on my knees and ask His help.

I went back to my little top-storey room in Northumberland Avenue. I read again through those four sheets of paper with the orders which someone, call Him God or what you will, had put into my mind so luminously that morning. I thought to myself, "Well, try anything once. If it doesn't work out, nobody need know. There's no harm done." Yet just the same there was that in me which said that if I did, even in the secrecy of my own clubroom, what my friend had suggested, things would never be the same with me again.

In that little top-storey room in Northumberland Avenue I got down on my knees. And I prayed something like this: "God, or whoever you are, if you are there, I will do what you tell me if you'll give me the strength to do it. But I can't do these things unless you help me."

Then I began to act on the instructions and thoughts which were written down on those four sheets of paper. I started putting right what I could of the wrongs I had done to others.

There was five pounds which I had "forgotten" to pay to the fellow who used to rub me down before Varsity matches at Oxford.

There was a much larger sum to restore to the Board of Education, who had partly financed my Oxford career in order that I should become a schoolmaster—which did not subsequently work out.

Then there were apologies—to Doë, as I have told, to my young brother and to people in the office. I had to say to a good many folk what Abraham Lincoln said publicly to one of his generals, "You were right. I was wrong. I'm sorry."

I saw clearly that only Christ could forgive, but only I could restore.

But I knew that if I did not fulfil my side of the contract, I could not expect God to step in and perform the miracle.

From that day habits went out of my life which I had believed were with me until I died.

To me the clinching evidence of God is the fact which I know from my own experience daily and constantly renewed, that there is a power available from outside ourselves to turn us into the sort of people all of us long to be—to give us a plan for our living beyond the limits of our human ambitions and desires, and to offer us the strength, wisdom and grace to live that plan.

From that moment in that tiny room in my club when for the first time in my life I decided to give God a chance, if He were there, to talk to me, to be really honest with myself about the things He said to me, my life has been transformed.

Do I mean that from that instant I became perfect? Of course not. Far from it. I stumble and grope my way along the thorny, narrow path which is marked by the bloodstained footprints of history. There are plenty of falls and many difficulties. Paul and Bunyan and many others wrote about that journey, charting the road for us ordinary men.

But I say this. Since I began to listen to God I have been given a new pace and purpose which puts the difficulties which once loomed so grey and grim into a fresh perspective.

It is an exhilarating human experience to be granted a sense of destiny, to be offered a distinctive place in a great and growing army marching under God to remake the world. Yet each of us can have it.

Since the day I made a start I have listened every morning, and many times in every day, and have never known God silent. This would have amazed me if you had told me about it some years ago. Yet it is simple enough. There is no mystery about it.

Throughout history men and women of every age have experienced the direction of God. Cromwell, Washington, Drake, Livingstone, Nightingale—for all of them it was the factor which added colour and courage to life. Abraham Lincoln, who listened to God at a time of crisis, and preserved a nation's unity, said, "I have so many evidences of God's direction that I cannot doubt this power comes from above. I am satisfied that when the Almighty wants me to do or not to do any particular thing, He finds a way of letting me know it."

And we do not need to be great statesmen like Abraham Lincoln before we can accept our share in the leadership of the new world order. For the ordinary man is the man of the future. It will be the ordinary men and women of many nations, empowered by a new force, a new passion, a new wisdom, who will provide the leadership to remake the world.

That is the destiny and tradition of true democracy which blossoms into glory, not under the leadership of towering individuals, but by the direction of inspired teams.

A determined minority of ordinary men and women, God-filled nobodies, will turn the tide of history.

CHAPTER XXII

SILVER THREAD

OUR inheritance has been built up and handed on to us by a race of fighters.

They fought the war of arms. Some lived. Some died in that war.

They fought the war of ideas. Some lived. Some died in that war too.

Through the ages of history the forces of Materialism have made their bid to overrun the world. In Britain the battle has often been in the balance. Yet, time and again, the Christian heritage has been preserved and enhanced by a fighting force of determined men.

After the fall of the Roman Empire, paganism engulfed the world, including Britain. It was then that our national greatness was founded by two groups of men who fought the war of ideas for Britain in a pincer movement from Scotland to Kent. They were led by Columba and Augustine. These men disagreed with each other in details, yet were allies in the war of ideas. They set out to capture the kingdom. They formed a plan. They drove out the pagan philosophy from the minds of the people, replacing it with a better big idea.

So within a few generations Britain was changed from an insignificant cluster of barbaric kingdoms into a nation whose Christian life and learning were a lamp for Europe.

Then came the counter-attack. The Norsemen invaded the country and almost overran it, bringing with them blood-worship and the cult of a super-race.

But Alfred was King in England. He was a far-sighted statesman.

He spent long hours every day seeking God's direction. His faith rings out across the centuries, "I say then, as say all good Christian men, that the divine purpose rules, and not fate."

He fought the war of arms and won it.

He fought the war of ideas and won it too. He converted the Danish King Guthrum to Christianity and stood godfather at his baptism. He captured the minds and wills of his enemies with a bigger idea than their own, after he had conquered their bodies in battle.

Sir Charles Oman in his history of England says, "Alfred made history. He was one of those rare spirits who actually turn back the flowing tide of circumstance and avert what seem to be inevitable conclusions. He was the first successful champion of Christian Europe against the all-pervading, all-conquering Viking swarm."

A new onslaught by the forces of Materialism followed the Renaissance. The Renaissance was a great new awakening in the spirit of man, but in many lands it degenerated into a throwback to pagan Materialism on a world front, where the beauty of the human form was represented as the supreme beauty and the human mind as the most powerful force in creation.

In England the war of ideas was fought and won by groups of devoted men. First Dean Colet, Sir Thomas More and Erasmus, centred in London and Oxford, raised a standard against the trends of their age. Some of them died for their faith. Then in Cambridge Tyndale and Coverdale held up the torch again.

These two groups of men, of different character and opposed to each other on certain issues, yet were dynamic and effective allies in the war of ideas. By the quality of their living and their enlightened strategy they were largely responsible for saving and developing the Christian tradition of the Renaissance in England. Without them the literature and courage of the Elizabethan era, with all its passion and fire and genius would have been impossible. Without them there might have been no Shakespeare, no Milton, no Cromwell and no Pilgrim Fathers.

From the spirit they spread grew the fighting faith of men like Drake and Howard of Effingham, who together turned back the Armada. Through them the Bible became the book of the people, the first and only book they ever had had. Its language became the language of the ordinary man of the day, and its basic philosophy was the accepted framework of all our national living.

Throughout British history, each clash-point of the war of ideas has been more than just another effort to save and preserve the existing Christian heritage. It is always the struggle as to whether a new stage and fresh step in man's journey shall be taken, or whether Britain shall be dragged back to the jungle.

The eighteenth century was a period of "reason" without religion. As the century moved on, moral decadence was reflected in the decadence of policy. We sank to a low ebb in our nationhood.

Temporarily the fire and genius of Chatham illuminated the darkness. But he had not the secret of the superforce of a new spirit. He did not understand how to produce the sustaining power for the whole nation. He could inflame enthusiasm but not inspire moral character. The bankruptcy of policy ended in the loss of the American colonies. So, less than 200 years ago, Materialism carved up an empire.

The Americans beat us in the war of arms. But the real defeat was in the war of ideas. The Americans had right on their side when they fought us. And we had no idea in our national life big enough to capture and hold the love of those who had founded a new world.

On top of all this Britain was, within a few years, involved in an ideological war on a world scale. We were confronted by a materialist revolution in France, a revolution of the Left, driving on towards world dictatorship in the name of Liberty, Equality and Fraternity, directed by the supreme military genius of the age.

Yet we beat Boney in a long drawn-out war. We went on to create what can prove to be the only enduring empire in history. Why?

The answer lies in the life and thinking of a group of men like Wesley and Wilberforce. They outmatched the oncoming forces of Materialism with the fire of a great awakening.

They carried our Christian heritage forward. They saved us from revolution and defeat. They built into the country the spiritual strength and moral toughness that gave it fighting endurance.

They fought the war of ideas to capture the thinking and living of the millions. Britain became an exporter of ideas as well as of goods. In the generations following Waterloo, Britain's ideas of Christian democracy and statesmanship, expressed in the great Trade Union movement, freedom from slavery and oppression, Parliamentary government, personal integrity and justice for all, helped to shape the lives of many countries and to give the force of a mighty idea to the Empire.

Before the last war, the reaction of Materialism began. Reaction is the right word. The "Isms" which in the name of Progress march mankind back towards the jungle are the most reactionary movements in history. The ideals of the past, rooted in our Christian faith, had been called in question by the big ideas of men like Voltaire, Thomas Huxley and Marx.

The years following 1918 found us at an ebb tide of our spiritual greatness as a nation.

So at the peace table, and after, we had nothing to give. We dictated peace terms which were terms of expediency rather than principle. In some cases, they were too hard. In other cases, they were too soft. Like all materialist remedies for moral ills, by themselves they did not work. We had no fighting faith to capture and inspire the vanquished.

We desolated them—we stripped them of their old allegiances and put nothing in their place. We left them bitter, cynical, a prey to Materialism, maimed and empty. Hitler stepped into a vacuum.

Meanwhile, we clung to watered-down Christianity and wishy-washy Materialism. So we were spiritually unprepared for the resumption of the struggle twenty years later. We had kept material comfort, and deprived our enemies of it. That toughened them and softened us.

We became spectators in a world swept by great tides of rival revolutionary philosophies. These tides still sweep on. They are ideas which spring in men's hearts and cannot be conquered on a battlefield.

Some hope that "moderates" will maintain stability in a world of warring ideologies. They are like the moderate sheep who thought she would maintain stability between the mad jackal and the angry wolf.

They are like the tipsy Irishman. He cycled home one dark night. He saw the lights of two bicycles coming towards him. "Sure, and I'll steer straight between 'em," says he. But they were the sidelights of a lorry.

To-day the liberating armies of the Allies are freeing the captives of Europe and Asia from their chains. But unless the liberating armies carry with them a liberating philosophy powerful enough to free men's minds, who can say what the next state of the world may be? There is an old story of the house which was swept and garnished —and because nothing occupied it, seven devils worse than the first took up their abode there. The last state of that house was worse than the first.

For a thousand years through storm and shine Britain has been shaped and steered by the most progressive and revolutionary idea so far produced to guide the thinking of mankind. It is the idea that true patriots are the men and women who accept a change of heart to meet the need of the future. That mankind is on the march and will become different—that it is not the destiny of human nature to remain the same throughout history.

> "Though we have stumbled,
> Yet through the darkness
> Runs the silver thread,
> Bright in the lives of men and women
> Who look fearless ahead.
> Men have served for Britain's glory,
> So may we bear on the story
> Of a Britain ever greater,
> Servant of God and man."

It will need a bigger idea than any "Ism" to outmarch the warring ideologies which bid for the world to-day. It will need the answering ideology, the big idea to outmatch both Left and Right with its passion, wisdom and power, to fire the minds of men to action and to change the motive of their hearts from Gimme to Give.

This is the future. It is backed by the superforce of God's living spirit. It is not a mingling of political programmes or a middle way between opposing groups of planners. It is an overarching and inspired way of life.

Chapter XXIII

ONCE TO EVERY MAN

SO we come to the end of our old journey, you and I together, and together we begin the new. We have never met before, and shall never part again. We can be numbered among the powerful of history. From this day we can march in the ranks of the swelling army of ordinary men and women whose destiny it is to make this nation and all nations greater.

Britain is a land of the past—and a land of the future too. There are so many things in her which touch the human heart to love. Both you and I, as we sit together and think of those things in that intimacy of the spirit which is ours, know parts of Britain, her sounds, her sights, her smells, which penetrate and stir the deepest corners of our nature.

Perhaps it is memories of the waters of Britain, the slick shadows of trout in tumbling streams, the slow and thoughtful glide of deeper rivers among the pasture land, and above all the sea, girdle and glory of our island, multitudinous, savage, restless, cold and grey and green, through centuries our shield and a challenge to the men of Britain's breed and race.

The sea which carried brave hearts to found an Empire and offered sanctuary to the Pilgrim Fathers on their inspired voyage to build a new world.

Perhaps it is the sound of laughter around a fireside, of country voices floating homeward across the field in summer dusk, when the last load of corn has been drawn into the stackyard and a mist is rising from the water-meadows; or the cough and whistle of wind in trees and around snug dwellings on a cold Christmas night.

Maybe we remember and love the spring-time valleys of white blossom furrowing the red earth of the West country, the grey moorland walls of the North with the granite of the hillsides and the warm hearts of the people, the smooth rounded downlands of the South with stub-faced sheep and white cliffs, or the arable earth of East Anglia, the ploughland of old England, with red poll beef and Suffolk punches heaving across the fen, their breath jutting before them from their nostrils like twin trumpets in the frosty air.

Maybe the thing which most catches our breath and heart is the subtle, simple smell of wood smoke on an autumn evening, that same smell which our island ancestors knew before the Romans came, and so from generation to generation.

All these things we inherit, you and I. And we inherit the green fields and thorn hedges and wild flowers, the treasures of the ages in literature and art, and above all the accumulated character and experience of a great people.

All these things are ours by right of legacy and life, no matter what circumstances surround us now, no matter if we spend our days in service of the Crown, at home or overseas, amid the stir of cities, in buses, tubes and trains, in black coats and bowler hats, in the sweat and danger of coal mines or the strain and clamour of factory or office or dock.

These things we have inherited. History will record what we make of our inheritance, you and I.

Many plan the future. But you and I live the future. We are the future.

For you and I, ordinary men and women, fellow-veterans of the shape of things to come, our frames dust and dirt and water, stirred with the same desires, wooed by the same temptations, borne forward by the same power if we choose, have this distinctive contribution to make.

We know the most precious secret of this and every generation, the secret which can remake the world. We possess the idea big enough to outmatch all other ideas, to mobilise the minds, hearts and wills of millions to unity and action.

Time is not on our side—unless we grasp it.

Tradition is not on our side—unless we live and create it.

God is not on our side—unless we listen and obey.

History will be written about the choice you and I make to-day. It will be the most momentous choice in human history.

For one thing is certain. We do stand on the threshold of a new age. A new age of some kind is about to be ushered in, with all the sweat and blood and agony of new creation.

It can be God's idea of a new age. If not, it will be a new age of another kind. And we, the ordinary men of our nation, sitting in our chairs to-day, we alone, the citizens of destiny, decide.

> "Once to every man and nation
> Comes the moment to decide.
> Then it is the brave man chooses
> While the coward stands aside,
> Till the multitude makes virtue
> Of the faith they had denied."